Conversations with a Blank Canvas

From Nowhere
to Somewhere
Decades of Change
and Transformation

Isa L Levy

ISBN: **9798652896898**

PAT DEVEREAUX
PUBLISHING WORKS
patdevereaux@mac.com

ACKNOWLEDGEMENTS

I would like to thank Joanna Godfrey Wood for her supportive contribution to editing my numerous drafts. I also extend my appreciation to Julia Hall for her consistent and patient listening which made my Life Story a possibility. I thank Pat Devereaux for enabling *"Conversations with a Blank Canvas"* to reach a larger audience than I could have anticipated; and I would also like to thank my friends and family past and present for teaching me invaluable lessons in the *"schoolroom of life".*

CONTENTS

Introduction   **Page 9**

Prologue: Who Am I?   **Page 13**

Decade 1: The Last Cry (1948/1958)   **Page 15**

Decade 2: Not Belonging (1958/1968)   **Page 28**

Decade 3: Into the Wilderness (1968/1978)   **Page 33**

Decade 4: Flowing (1978/1988)   **Page 41**

Decade 5: Growing (1988/1998)   **Page 47**

Decade 6: Belonging (1998 / 2010)   **Page 54**

Decade 7: Speaking from the Heart (2008/2018)   **Page 74**

Interlude: Pause For Thought (Christmas 2017)   **Page 82**

Decade 8: Life Unfolding (2018…)   **Page 86**

Epilogue: Female Resurrection   **Page 94**

References   **Page 97**

About the Author   **Page 98**

Book Reviews   **Page 100**

Copyright   **Page 103**

Conversations with a Blank Canvas

In this memoir I would like to share some of the evolutions I have lived through in the process of becoming my True Self, having started my life as a rank outsider in so many ways. Some of these evolutions included actor, artist, arts psychotherapist, *lost child*, *lost adolescent* and *lost woman*. In so doing, I reveal how I journeyed from a False Self to a more *authentic* one, a condition I see in my work as an arts psychotherapist, often thinly disguised beneath a veil of depression, anxiety and loneliness, or what I call the "blank canvas," where words may not easily be found.

In the first two decades, I describe what conditions contributed to my False Self and how in the next two decades I take on the role of "actor" in both my personal and professional life while connecting to my True Self in my fifth decade while facing an actual blank canvas in my studio – a process that finally led to my signature painting "The Female Resurrection,"

Connecting with my creative self-expression has held my sanity in check throughout the decades, although I cannot deny how difficult this journey has been. I describe how, during my fifth decade, I paint some 450 paintings, without having had any prior art experience. How in my early 60s I complete a Masters Degree in Arts and Psychotherapy, having failed academically throughout my schooling; and how I have a whole new career as an arts psychotherapist in my seventh decade. In my eighth decade, I end up back on stage in a musical production based on Susie Orbach's book Fat is A Feminist Issue and receive an invitation from my local MP to sing a song in Parliament I wrote some 50 years ago on the subject of the climate crisis, although having no conscious idea at the time that this subject would become a future emergency.

Conversations with A Blank Canvas is a story about change and evolution in which I strive to offer motivation and hope for healing and transformation to others. In brief, you could say that it's a celebration of life, complexity and freedom.

In coming to terms with the trauma in my own personal and cultural history I can find my voice at long last when for so long the *authentic* me had been invisible and silenced in the effort to fit in and belong within the cultural and female roles expected of me, and yet not being able to do so. All the feelings, true and false, are held within the fabric of the "blank canvas". However I never compromised my life in this respect and this book shows my unique journey to live my *authentic* life, although against the tide, especially at the time of my birth just after the Second World War. I hope to pass on how I crossed the frontier of negative belief structures, often played out in the shape of depression and anxiety, disconnection and loneliness; a feeling of deeply held unworthiness at the core of my being that led to such low self-esteem and lack of confidence. I show how I lived through, developed and transcended my personal history by eventually accepting and releasing my emotionally impoverished and strangulated True Self from invisibility.

Through sharing my life story I hope that my insight and understanding can be of help to readers on what might lie hidden behind the guise of their own "blank canvasses". I am compelled to share this so that others might find the courage to lead more *authentic* lives, with more insight into their inner landscapes and what feels *authentic* for them, rather than habitually recreate the lives that others expect of them or they of themselves, without reflection. This is becoming ever more vital with the *selfie* epidemic of fabricated, superficial false images, based on how you look, leading a younger generation to feel increasingly at sea, insecure, disconnected and isolated from their "true selves," where all the positive self-empowerment lies; and in the process creates a pursuit of something that doesn't exist and an increase in mental health problems on an epidemic scale.

Introduction

Voice of the "Artist"

Writing this is an impossible mission. How can you describe the "indescribable"? And yet it befalls me to try. Why? Because what lays hidden within the "blank" holds the answers! Can this be put into words? No. So I am on a mission to fail but this will not stop me, for my "artist's voice" has a singular thread to it which is a magic pull from the material to the mysterious.

Why did I appear before an audience wearing a bare set of exposed plastic boobs, delivering a lecture on the meaning of life? It was a need to expose that what might be viewed superficially, could be a screen to something far more interesting and complex.

And so I listened, finally, to two clairvoyants who said I had to write my life story; one some forty years ago and one altogether more recent. I can sincerely say that I would not have started writing without this prompting. My life story is not something that I find at all easy to put into words as, in a way, I like the mystery of the invisible, of the "not knowing", with certainly no absolutes along the way. Freedom and personal space is my sanctuary, which is possibly the opposite of how our Western world functions and which was certainly not a part of my early environment and upbringing.

So the "blank canvas" for me represents a personal inner sanctuary in which, within the stillness, I can hear a very small voice beneath the thunder of the day-to-day world ringing its truth; a heart-awakening, if you like, to the way forward, even if it says "no". These are faint murmurings which direct me on my next path without knowing why or what might be the consequences. I just follow, trusting that it's meant for a reason that I am unaware of.

If we take the writing of this memoir I knew that I had something to share, but I did not know that the one I needed to share it with was myself. For even though I have lived through the evolutions that I have, and my life has been a rather strange and diverse one for a woman of my years, I was a mystery to myself and had not been able to process my experiences sufficiently, so that the core of me could have a home. My writing has helped with this process and I am visible now, a lot more visible, which heralds a place of "homecoming".

Because I was a daydreamer when I was in the educational system I can speak from a position of understanding about not fitting into that world, or any other for that matter; it's a natural state to fit in and belong and a very painful one not to do so. As I write this introduction, new words are entering our vocabulary via the celebrity culture: *"self-partnering,"* the latest definition to explode forth – and identified as – *"a person who would feel whole and fulfilled within the **self** and does not feel compelled to seek fulfilment through having another person as a **partner"**.* I am rather glad that in some way there is a word, to sum up how I feel.

So who am I? And where do I fit in? These are questions I have asked throughout my life and realise now that it doesn't matter, because I am breathing and alive and in that, I am a precious human being, living on planet earth, in this day and age as all others are, also. Some of us sadly live in dire poverty and cruel war situations while others of us live where material comforts are a given and yet still cannot know happiness and contentment. It is impossible to make sense of this and accept the world as it is if we dwell too much on it, which we do.

I have always been searching and scratching beneath the surface for a connection that was deeper than what I witnessed around and beyond me. The realm of creative expression has helped me on my spiritual quest in which, for some brief moment, all the dots seem to join up; where there could be harmony and balance; a natural feel of grace, beauty, ugliness, chaos, order, containment, joy, dance and rhythm within that incompleteness.

Voice of the "Blank Canvas"

When I faced the blank canvas for the first time in my studio and shut the door on the world, it was a particularly messy time in my life, in the wake of my mother's death. I had no idea of what to paint or any background or training in painting but that's what made it so refreshing. I knew nothing, so I could go anywhere because I did not know; that was my freedom. Spreading, sculpting the paint, the smell, the colours and textures blending, seeping and bleeding into each other; shapes were appearing with the rhythm of e – motion (energy in motion). Then I followed the painting's development like a servant follows its master or mistress, breathing the painting to life.

Within that, however, I met my demon spirits trying to destroy my attempts with a punitive, negative critique: "Do you call this art? Who do you think you are? You know nothing. What is it? This isn't pretty. It's not accurate. It's a mess!" But for once I would not be put off by this critical voice because I knew that what I felt was a real connection with the deepest part of me: my mind, body, soul and spirit were speaking and I was refusing to listen to that self-deprecating voice. I wasn't at all interested in accuracy anyhow; spontaneity was an *authentic* gift, where I could find a sense of grace, celebration and harmony within the process of filling in each blank canvas.

And so the blank canvas was my friend, accepting the whole experience of being "me", sometimes even including a little accuracy in my portraits and life studies, but not enough to kill my free spirit. I was flying and it wasn't a short-term romance – it was my flowering, coming to life as my *authentic* self; flowing; accepting mistakes as places of focus for energy that created something I would never have known before. This was the mystery that I had always been looking for but was also far removed from. I learnt so much from this experience and painted so many paintings that after a while there was nothing left for me to do but to *stop* and open the door onto the world again with all the knowledge that I had learnt in the process.

Voice of the "Therapist"

So I opened the door onto what?… I had found my way to something through the realm of my painting, but in terms of understanding my evolution through the experience, I could not. This is what must have propelled me into the therapist world, because in training for my masters in arts and psychotherapy I was really finding answers to what it was to be human, as I often felt like an alien, somewhat lost on this earthly plain. A part of me was avidly keen to find answers and I had discovered more clarity through my work and training as an arts psychotherapist as to why I was such an alien to myself. I discovered that I'm not alone in putting on a show or front to the world, which makes us feel more confident and acceptable, but is, in reality "false", allowing us to think that we have life *sorted*, when in real terms we have denied other significant parts of ourselves. I now know that listening and giving a voice to all the different parts of myself, hidden or otherwise, actually makes me a healthier human being, as I can engage with the voices that have been silenced. In my own case the creative part of "me" was my visible "uniform" to the world, hiding all other insecurities and riches within the blank canvas.

I can now see how I would have been attracted to arts psychotherapy as a therapeutic training, as it embraced the total potential of being human; not only words, but creative expression, not a "blank screen" therapist but a living and real therapeutic relationship; not only the practical day-to-day life skills, behaviours, mood management, but the power of the imagination and the spirit in searching the heart and soul where words are often non-existent.

I have found that the fear of breaking down defences is the greatest fear of all. What if I am awful, terrible, horrible, incapable – and all the other negatives? My question would be what if you found yourself to be only partly awful, terrible, horrible, incapable – then what?

This is why I find my work as an arts psychotherapist so fascinating. Each time I meet with a client is a dip into the mystery that often there is so much more than there appears to be. Working with a client is like a growing piece of art – we are in the process of together crafting a life in the shared therapeutic space, often witnessing life becoming fuller, richer and more meaningful, which is very good news indeed. Human reactions to all that life has to offer from love to tragedy, success, confusion, chaos, traumatic responses to fear and all the emotional complexities that we as mortals have to navigate.

When I first set out on the path of writing this memoir I intended to underpin my life experience from the standpoint of Donald Winnicott's True Self/False Self theory. Winnicott was a child psychiatrist working in the 1950s who came up with this theory. His premise was that the True Self was the flowing spontaneous part of the "self", which has an instinctive quality of truthful engagement in the present moment of our lives and events, which facilitates our capacity to find a way to deal authentically with the circumstances that we find ourselves in. The "False Self", however, has learnt to mould itself to life's circumstances from an adaptive stance that is more negatively reactive to experiences – trying to fit in, to be liked, for example, or loved, rescued or left alone. I chose this theory as I felt that I fitted into it since I had learnt to be an actor both professionally and personally, learning to pretend, lost to my True Self. I believe that the True Self has a multitude of colours and dimensions. It is like the conductor of a symphony, raising its baton to the softer voices and evoking the subtleties, calming the raucous screeches of the out-of-tune violins, consoling the sobbing "child" oboe that thinks it should be a grown-up bassoon and subduing the fearful angst-ridden soprano who is neurotically attached to being an angst-ridden soprano. Such is the challenge of the True Self, which has the power to discern and reflect, protect and initiate while lying at home within the "self", the "self" that can tolerate just how wretched and beautiful a symphony life can be.

Prologue

(Who Am I?)

Female

Jew

Self-Partnered

Hospital Receptionist

Non-Conformist Mystic

Actor Comedy / Tragedy

Singer /Songwriter / Guitarist

Sales Person (sold everything from encyclopaedias to advertising space;

but never managed to sell a kitchen)

Time-Share Sales; Portugal / Spain

Visual Artist / Painter / Digital / Fashion

Arts Workshops Children / Adults

Nursing Home Activities Organiser

MAM – MA with Merit

Arts Psychotherapist

Poet

Film Documentary Subject

Writer (and more …)

into the unknown I leap and leap into the core of

WHO I AM

and who I am not…

*"**A Magical Mystery Tour**"*

Decade 1: The Last Cry

(1948/1958)

I remember the brown flock wallpaper and the small bedroom where my cot faced the window, and where the door was placed in relation to my cot. I was approximately one year old, and I remember the "last cry" I made before I took an unconscious decision to keep my distress to myself. To me it felt as if I had been crying forever, and I was alone and isolated in a big world, where no one came to comfort me in my boredom and distress; no one seemed to care. My parents were socialising in a downstairs room and I don't remember crying again until I was nine-years-old, after I had been removed from my ballet class. Now, looking back on those early days I can see how important it was to fit in with the family culture and expectations, but now, seventy years on, I realise that although being a *good girl* won me a sense of belonging, it was to the detriment of a more *authentic* or *true* self that remained hidden within the fabric of my "blank canvas". My father's mother had died when he was 18-months-old and his chaotic family background had created much unhappiness for him, causing him to run away and join his elder brother in London, prior to the second world war, in which he had fought as an RAF pilot. I can now see how the security of a military regime, with clear rules and regulations, could have been a comfort to him and how this might have influenced the tight and rigid control he had established over the family; however this is not the whole story, by any means, as he could also be great fun and also the more "maternal" of my parents.

I was born in Cardiff in the aftermath of the war. Before meeting my father, my mother had not been without a suitor, however he had been non Jewish and this was not an acceptable option, the Rabbi being called in to put an end to it. My mother's mother was suffering from Parkinson's disease and I think my mother had fully convinced herself that she would never marry, as 28-years-old was considered to be a late age to marry in those days.

When my father came on the scene, a handsome young man in his airforce uniform and proposed marriage to my mother, I imagine my mother and her family were both shocked and delighted. After a three-week courtship they were married in Belfast in 1946 but on the very same day of their marriage my father's father died, so this was a very sad beginning to the marriage. My father was not altogether a stranger to my mother's family, for my father's sister had married my mother's brother; and so it was brother and sister marrying brother and sister.

My mother uprooted from her native Belfast to set up home in Cardiff with my father, who at that time was living with his step-mother, a not a very popular woman by all accounts, and who I only met once. This was quite enough as she offered some critical comment about my teeth protruding – not at all reassuring for an eight-year-old who was beginning to be self-conscious about the way she looked. My other grandparents had died before I was born and I only met my maternal grandmother once, when I was three years old; she was already suffering from Parkinson's disease, and so my early childhood was somewhat bereft of warm, emotional, connections. My father's rules were to be obeyed, and there were punishments for not doing so, and I was fearful of making mistakes and being on the receiving end of his anger. So compliance was a better option but it was at the expense of hiding and silencing my own wishes and needs.

My mother's father was a Polish immigrant who had settled in Belfast, where he had some relatives. Although not at first being able to read or write, he later went on to create a successful business in retail furniture and produced a family of five children: three boys and two girls.

The male siblings took an active role in the family business and the girls were expected to marry. My mother, the youngest, was referred to as "the ugly duckling" in the wake of her glamorous sister, who looked like a 1940s film star, who would be taken around the world by her father, and who ended up in finishing school in Switzerland, while my mother cared for her sick mother. I can only imagine how this must have impacted on my mother's confidence and self-esteem. Also, perhaps more significantly, she was told by her parents that she was a "mistake", having been conceived accidentally on a weekend away. Her siblings would gladly echo these cruel sentiments. For example, as a small child, trying to climb onto the settee, her siblings would shout out: "Get off, you're a mistake!" This must have made her feel an extreme sense of rejection and pain, and made her feel so unwelcome in life, contrary to what should have been a loving and caring environment.

I was born into the background of my parent's unresolved traumas – as neither had had their basic needs met in a warm, supportive or encouraging home life and I believe they suffered a disproportionate sense of hurt that had to be hidden within the "blank canvas"; neither had received positive emotional connections or care in their own backgrounds. As a sensitive child, I picked up what couldn't be shared in words or emotions and felt the need for something that I could not express. Now I know that it was the need for love and connection and an expression of my warm and caring, spontaneous, feelings that would surface, only to be repressed again. Sometimes my father was very present in this way, but sadly my mother was too deeply wounded to have any space in her internal world of emotions to possess a capacity to relate to children in the way a child needs. Empathetic was not how you would describe my mother.

My father was a young, Welsh, published poet, prior to the war, who had exchanged poetry with the Welsh poet, Dylan Thomas. My father's family were from Swansea, as

MY PARENTS ON THEIR WEDDING DAY

was Dylan Thomas. My father's brother, the art critic and writer, Mervyn Levy, had shared a Chelsea home with Dylan Thomas.

I have a letter written to my father from Dylan Thomas asking "Are there were any more poems growing in Nab Valley?" My father's title for his own anthology of poems called – "Nab Valley", an anagram of his name, Alban Levy. After the war, on the strength of this, he was admitted to study English literature at the University of Wales in Cardiff.

At the time of my birth in 1948 my father was studying and times were hard financially, as there was no income. Those early days must have been traumatic for my mother, coming from a fairly well-off family in Belfast, and with no other life experience to serve as a comparison. They lived with my father's step-mother.

My mother talked of how his step-mother made soup from the juice of a can of peas. This must have been an incredible shock for my mother, whose culinary skills were instilled in her by her Austrian mother. My mother boasted that she and her sister could pluck and steam a chicken from the age of three. Food and the kitchen were what she was most familiar with and where she was most at home. So all her maternal efforts went into food and shopping and the preparation of plenty of it. As far as my mother was concerned, food was love.

This has been a major problem in my own life, since food and a struggle with my weight has been a long legacy. When I was a small baby I did not want to eat at the set mealtimes but I was forced to do so by my parents. They distracted me by lighting matches and then pushing the food into my mouth, so I'm told, where the food stayed lodged in my cheeks, until the next meal, when I would spit it out.

My father was brought up by maids and nannies (and their boyfriends) in a wild and chaotic environment where he and his siblings would run wild. His step-mother did not care for children. It's easy to see how rules mattered to him when he joined the air force and later on in our family home. He was shattered by his childhood and was painfully shy, with a stammer. His elder brother Mervyn was a bohemian artist, and by all accounts quite a character, getting his younger siblings to attempt dangerous pranks. One such prank was to tie various scarves together, linking the upstairs to the downstairs, over three floors. Then asking for a volunteer to check the robustness of the cradle seat. My father's sister happily agreed to take up the challenge and ended up stuck between floors, with no one attempting to rescue her. All were screaming out "Stella come this way, not that way", so I'm told. Finally the cradle disintegrated and fell to the ground taking my aunt with it and breaking her arm in the process.

My uncle was very much the "black sheep" of the family and in this I find identification with him. I think my father found him a strange, mad specimen, as did the extended family, for he did not live his life according to traditional family values or expectations. I saw him very rarely, only two or three times in my life. He was marginalised by the family; not that I think it worried him too much, as he had a successful television career in presenting a "painting for all' art series. He published books on art and artists in many different languages. He also taught drawing at the Royal College of Art. I, however, regret that I didn't get to know my uncle, as I suspect we had a lot in common.

My parents were very prominent in the Cardiff Jewish community. In that close-knit environment anyone not toeing the line would stand out. I learnt to smile and fit in and knew no other way of conducting myself. My mother's slogan GBI or "grin and bear it" became a family mantra… and so I did. I also learnt to make people laugh. I actually remember doing so as a little baby in my pram, when being told to "smell the pretty flowers" and making a funny face that made the adults laugh so much that my aunt peed herself. Not surprising, then, that I became a comedy actress.

BABY IN A BOTTLE

PLAYING WITH A TIN BOX

When I was two my brother was born. He suffered from bad asthmatic attacks. I remember seeing the oxygen cylinders being dragged into the bedroom and being frightened by my brother's screams as I watched and waited on the stairs, alone, as he underwent painful injections. I thought he might die, which thankfully, was not the case.

Wales being the "land of song" influenced me profoundly, in terms of song and my love of singing, something which has continued throughout my life. I would orchestrate sing-songs, before my brother and I fell asleep. In the small bedroom we shared, one bunk bed on top of the other, I sang with much more gusto and enthusiasm than he, I'm told. My father and I would enjoy singing Welsh folk songs together while drying up the dishes, in between my brother and I would be licking water at each other. We got five shillings a week pocket money, but pennies were deducted for bad behaviour, my father kept a tab on money deducted for telling tales, burping, saying shut up or the like.

There were many interesting characters, including uncles and aunts, who came to stay and I remember observing, with humour, a colourful array of larger-than-life theatrical characters appearing on my doorstep, with my parents offering their extravagant hospitality and liveliness. I, being more of an observer than a participant in life, enjoyed the display of such lively people, often Eastern European Jewish refugees, who had started up businesses in the Welsh valleys after escaping the Holocaust.

I was at school in the fifties, just after the war. I remember queuing for milk tablets, since milk was rationed, but I do not remember being involved in lessons in any way that I found engaging. I spent most days gazing out of the window onto the playing fields and into the gardens and homes of other families. I can see now that this escaping from reality was something that was an unconscious mechanism that Winnicott would call "primary dissociation", to relieve boredom and a feeling of "greyness" that might well have augmented my creative needs to make reality more colourful and interesting but it did not leave me well versed for passing exams.

I was brought up at a time when corporal punishment was permitted in schools and I saw other children having their hands hit with a ruler. I did not endure this mistreatment but was the recipient of a smack from my father when I accidentally spilt or broke something and my father's raised voice was shock enough to cause me to pee myself. I felt humiliation at not being able to control my body as well as shame at spilling or dropping things and displeasing my father.

When I was nine and coming up to the Eleven-Plus, it was noted that I was falling behind and I was taken out of my ballet class to engage in some private coaching. I remember sobbing as I was driven away from the last ballet class. I had loved it so much. It was a world that I could fit into; a world of music, harmony, routines, concerts, grace, and coordination, and just like that, it was taken away from me without any concern for my feelings.

My father by this time had qualified as a teacher but finances were still low, so much so that my mother talked of my father cutting out paper pelmets from newspapers to top up our curtains, as real ones were unaffordable.

My mother wanted to prove to her family that she could be financially independent and so set up her own retail shops. Three in fact over the years, selling toys, haberdashery, wool and wallpaper in the different shops that became so much part of our lives. My father, by this time a lecturer, would at the end of his college day go to the shop to cash up. We were raised by maids and nannies that I did not bond with, however, I was curious about this array of young women from different parts of Europe and had a taste for the European Union long before its declaration. It did, however, educate me in what seemed to me to be an exotic difference and I was fascinated by this. I remember the maid's room as being dark and depressing.

Later in my teenage years, when the *au pairs* were dispensed with, it became mine and I could choose my own colours – orange, hessian, wall-paper and a little sink of my own – a sort of "home from home". I was beginning to find an *authentic* connection to my True Self, where colour and a natural sense of harmony formed my own pleasing world.

Winding back a few years, I believe what could not be expressed in the way of grief at both my parents' losses, was possibly *my* emotional inheritance. With my father's father dying on his wedding day and my mother's mother dying when I was aged three, there were a lot of unshed tears. I remember my mother being taken off in an ambulance in the wake of her mother's death. I imagine she suffered a nervous breakdown, although it was never openly talked about and I was never able to verify it. I do remember being taken in by a neighbour and seeing the ambulance drive away, with my mother in it, as I pretended to help our neighbour do the dusting. This event was never talked about again and my mother was absent for what seemed a very long time. I have a letter that my father wrote to my mother during this time saying how heartbroken he was when I asked: "Where's Mummy?"

It seems to me, in retrospect, that both my parents dealt with pain through denial. Both were very charismatic and could hide behind the screen of a warm, sociable and hospitable front, which made them very popular in the community. At home, however, it was rather different. It felt emotionally cold, bleak and regimented when my parents were not entertaining others. Although, my father would play with us, tell us stories while putting us to bed and bathing us. My father was a complex character, caring and fun most of the time, but sometimes angry and lashing out, which was confusing for me. Fun times happened most especially in the garden, where we had made a small golf course, digging holes into the lawn, playing cricket with the neighbourhood kids in regular tournaments and my father taking the role of umpire.

My mother was not present at play times, except when we could hold a hand-of-cards, we would play with matches as stakes until we had gathered enough pocket money to play with real money, which made us feel very grown up. She loved playing occasional games of poker with the men and I think she probably preferred the company of men to women. She proudly declared that she would put a bet on two flies climbing the wall .Most Saturday evenings were spent playing Kalooki with my parents' friends, a 13-card type of rummy. I thought, in those days, that I would have reached maturity the day I could hold 13 cards in one hand like the adults.

She had a strong physical presence and always had a story to tell friends and strangers. These events put herself centre stage, not only in her own world, but always encouraging others to join her in the drama of what she would describe as an *hysterical* event, when in reality it was just an ordinary encounter but to her it was *hysterical*. This added sense of drama was captivating to her audience, possibly enhancing the theatrical part of myself.

Although my father was a stickler for rules my mother seemed at odds with this concept, most especially concerning the authority of traffic wardens or the police, where these established rules did not seem to apply to her, or so she thought. In one incident, I was her passenger on a car journey through the country lanes of Cardiff. She was a speedy driver, always going over the speed limit, as patience and caution were not part of her mind-set. On this occasion she noticed she was being followed by a police car and knew also that a few more penalty points would likely cause her disqualification, so she accelerated, as did the police car. Eventually she ground to a halt and jumped out of the car with a hugely dramatic performance, declaring great relief that it was the police, as she thought she was being followed. The police were quite distracted by her Oscar-winning performance, as was I, and they let her off.

Other incidents included the world of traffic wardens; my mother's idea was that they should look after her car while she ran off to do her shopping, even though she was illegally parked. This worked most times except on one occasion, when she had parked between the studs of a zebra-crossing, and she returned to find that she had been booked. Others might have paid the fine without resistance but my mother decided to fight the case in the courts declaring that she wasn't inside the studs. This was an opportunity for the whole family to witness my mother in the box. It was more like going to the theatre than anything else, certainly, it was a unique experience. The judge, however, not so entertained, asked why she thought the police officer was taking her address. "Was it to send you a Valentine card Mrs Levy?" She was fined accordingly, yet still holding that it was the policeman's word against hers and her own verdict remained "not guilty".

She held onto her opinions and I remember how challenging it was to engage in an ordinary conversation with her as she was very much in her own world and not prepared or able to allow any new information in. So conversation, with talking and responsive listening, was really difficult and I had to deaden my True Self in the wake of that as any *authentic* connection was an impossibility. There were times when she and I would take walks around the park and have an ice-cream together, these were mutually enjoyable times, but I don't think she felt she could relax in these leisure moments. She would sit on the edge of her seat – always ready to go … somewhere else. This, quite naturally, affected me. Why could she not spend enjoyable quiet times with me? Was I not worth it? I now understand how her huge physical presence was a cover-up for a vulnerable inner world that needed protection. My mother's inner world, which I could not reach, propelled me with a compulsive drive to search for what couldn't be articulated out loud – a world of connection and emotional richness and expression. So my creativity was a life-saver for me and this has taken me through the decades. I now see that what was denied me behind the "blank canvas" of my mother's deadened emotional world was what kept me searching for clues to the everyday palette of emotional expression. This could not be reached in any other way for me, but through the spirit of music, drama, art and spirituality.

At age three I began ballet classes and loved that world of music and expression that seemed in some way to make sense to me. I felt an *authentic* relationship within myself. I was not a brilliant little dancer but I felt at home in the class and I enjoyed being an "elf" at a performance in the New Theatre in Cardiff. This was not an altogether successful endeavour, for when I thought I was running behind the backcloth to get to the other side of the stage, I found myself to be a "lone elf" on a huge, completely empty, stage, with teachers on either side, telling me to "get off". I could hear my mother's voice saying: "It's Isa". I was paralysed with fear and humiliation, not knowing which direction to take, while being so visible and exposed. Although I so enjoyed my ballet class by the end of primary school I was taken out of the class to have extra tuition for the 11 Plus as I was falling behind in school. I remember the last ballet class so well as I sat in the back of our large van with the ballet teacher, Miss Dando, sobbing my heart out, as I had had no idea this was to be my last class. I think I lost all sense of what I enjoyed being a part of my life from then on and developed a sense of "powerlessness" as if I didn't exist while the world within and without fell away.

However, going back to the beginning of primary school, I enjoyed reading and writing and one of my hand-embroidered mats ended up on display at the Royal Bath and West Show, maybe another early indication of my creative expression getting an audience. Most other school experiences remained lost in a fog. However, I enjoyed playing the

THREE YEAR OLD BALLERINA

recorder and took part in concerts. On one such occasion my mother found herself sitting behind a very tall man. From the stage, I could see her standing and waving at me, in a Joanna Lumley, *Ab Fab* manner, which I found most embarrassing, but she would, sadly, have been oblivious to my feelings. After the show, rather than talking about my part in the concert, she talked about the tall man sitting in front of her, without acknowledging my performance. This left me feeling insignificant and invisible.

I also remember hearing short excerpts of *Under Milk Wood* at school, which fuelled my imagination, perhaps punctuated by the fact that Dylan Thomas stayed with the family when I was two and I sat on his lap, so the story goes. My mother asked him what he'd like for breakfast, he replied: "A pint of beer, Lily me darling" and she said: "What else, Dylan?" and he said: "another pint of beer, Lily me darling…" with a very good Irish accent, mimicking my mother. This was probably not well received by my mother as her breakfasts were to die for and my cousins still, to this day, talk about these large, sumptuous feasts. Food, however, was not a notable feature of Dylan's menu…

Both my parents worked and played hard and were prominent in the Cardiff Jewish community. On evenings when my parents were in, we would sit in the lounge watching the telly and eventually, when my mother did sit down in her favoured armchair, having spent time in the kitchen (her favourite place), she would join us and fall asleep as soon as her body hit the chair. I remember one hot summer's Sunday afternoon, her being fast asleep in the garden in her armchair, as we played loudly by her side. Sleeping was my mother's way of dealing with manic activity, which she excelled at…

Sometimes on a Wednesday, which was a half-day for the shop, we would be collected from school and taken off to the beach, which was always a great treat. On Sundays we would roll up in our Ford Transit van (for shop deliveries) to our favourite destination, Porthcawl, Southerndown, or Barry Island, and there we consumed a large picnic. The food was enough for many more than our own party and my mother would always try to include others in our flock – as it always had to be, for her, more than just the family. This was because social life was far more interesting than the family, as she could play to a bigger audience.

Often on holidays I would join my cousins in Belfast or they would come to Cardiff and we would go off to funfairs, parks and on country walks. We also helped out in the shop, my brother and I were always on call on Saturdays and during the holidays, in our adolescent years. I did not mind too much as I could be an observer of others in between serving the customers. However, my mother would keep me on my toes and idle moments of observation would have to be filled by tidying shelves or looking busy at least.

And so I approached the end of my first decade lost to my *authentic* self, feeling only that I wanted to blend in and belong, yet feeling so much that I didn't.

'Missing the fit ... I am different, I am other. Perhaps there is, at some point in life, a sense of pride in not belonging, or in belonging in a different way. But for the most part, there is only a sense of distance between yourself and the sea of other people who fit ... '

The Misfit's Manifesto, Yuknavitch, L. (2017)

Matching my parents charisma and charm – I could not. I felt as though I was under their spell but with a feeling of personal isolation. My inner world was on hold. This being so, pretending became a sense of achievement and success to my False Self. On the other hand, I was fostering, festering, feelings underneath this shell of protection as I approached the Eleven-Plus and the beginning of my next decade. I faced an inner world of "greyness" that had to be hidden.

Decade 2: Not Belonging

(1958/1968)

This decade begins with my failing the Eleven-Plus at the same time as gaining weight, both attributing to poor feelings of self-esteem and an embarkation onto the first of my weight-loss programmes. My mother accompanied me on these ordeals, always ready to alert me that my appearance was below par and that I should wear a corset, or elasticated pantihose that would hide the fat, but only pushed it somewhere else, to my mind. All in all, the whole thing was a miserable experience and plagued a central part of my inner life during the tender years of adolescence. I felt so out of control in it all, and this exacerbated feelings of isolation, low self-confidence and a feeling a failure, not only in school, but also in how I looked.

I did not fit into the school system and remember my second year as being the worst; my school report revealing no subject higher than 20 percent. I felt exposed, as if everyone could see how badly I was doing, and I felt a deep sense of shame, terrified of showing my father my report, which, at least, did not create the response I had expected, as he seemed none too concerned at this juncture and life continued… without any comment from him. It was I who held the shame.

There were positives however, in attending a secondary modern school, which would not have been awarded me had I been at a grammar school and these positives were a life-saver for me.

Drama, which I happened to excel at, maybe the only thing, became a tangible cord I could hold onto, as I won the junior drama prize, which was at least something positive and concrete in my life.

Here, at long last, was an opportunity for me to find a creative outlet for my inner world, which was something that gave me a little more confidence and could make others laugh. Although I did not fit into the academic school requirements, I did have some unique talent that had been noticed, which gave me some sort of direction. I surmise that had I been at a grammar school I would not have discovered this talent. Making others laugh, as I seemed able to do, was an aphrodisiac to me, much as it had been for me as a baby. There was definitely a stronger focus on drama and music in my secondary modern school than there might have been had I gone to a grammar school and I excelled in both subjects. I now believe that I needed some sort of experiential engagement with a subject to be interested. Not only was I awarded the junior drama prize but also the senior music prize. My confidence grew in the wake of these worlds opening to me – as concrete manifestations that I could be "seen", and had been rewarded, in the wake of my academic failures.

On the strength of this, I sought part-time drama classes at the Welsh College of Music and Drama situated in Cardiff Castle, which was a very welcome Saturday morning excursion, after which I would head off by bus to my parents' shop to help out. I remember on the bus ride to the shop a recurrent feeling of depression as I passed by an area in Cardiff full of large, modern and soulless houses, thinking that I would live there with my husband, possibly a lecturer, in what would appear to be an outward manifestation of a successful life, while feeling inwardly emotionally starved.

I would have liked to learn the piano but my parents thought I would not persevere with piano lessons and declined my request, so I took up the classical guitar instead and also started singing lessons at this time. These both boded well and stood me in good stead for a future in theatre, as these skills could be useful additions to my career as an actress, although I did not realise that at the time. I was quite inhibited by art in the classroom as I never felt I knew what to do and my father and brother would do my homework for me. My often strange attempts at paintings were amusing to my father, and so I held that I was pretty hopeless.

At the age of 14 I was hospitalised with appendicitis and enjoyed my time there as a patient in the women's ward, gaining special attention from the women who took pity on me, as the youngest. I felt much looked after by the women patients. This experience might well have fostered an interest I was to follow a few years later, along the path of a career in hospital administration.

At the same age I had my first encounter with the opposite sex and engaged in my first kiss in a flea-pit cinema in Blaenclydach, a blind date arranged by a friend of my parents, whose nephew was arriving from London with a friend. Myself and another girlfriend were invited to meet with them. We travelled all the way through the Welsh Valleys from Cardiff to meet these two Londoners. I remember it as being not an altogether pleasurable experience, trying to wash the kiss away as soon as I got home. Other teenage encounters happened in the Jewish Youth Club attached to the darkened Synagogue. I found these escapades quite an ordeal as I was rather disengaged.

At aged 15 I endured my Bat Mitzvah along with my brother, who was 13, having his Bar Mitzvah at the same time. Girls were deemed to mature later, so it fitted in very well that it could be a joint affair. I was excruciatingly self-conscious, feeling very out of place, as friends and family gathered from all over the globe with all eyes on me, I felt. I was dressed all in white, with a stiff white trilby hat and feelings that were even stiffer; I remember also, that it was the one time in my life that I could not contain my emotions and the tears rolled down my cheeks after I read my portion from the Talmud, the Jewish Law. I would have liked the ground to swallow me up. Also, on reflection, I was

Photos

MY BROTHER AND I IN THE '60S

finding the relentless partying throughout the weekend pretty unbearable, but without consciously knowing it.

As I look back, I realise that I was also feeling traditional religion hard to bear. I used to spend most synagogue time, as a child, plaiting my father's prayer shawl and observing those around me. The emphasis on the social aspect of the religious community, and during my Bat Mitzvah, left me feeling uncomfortable, although it is only now in writing over the past few years that I realise how against the grain this all was for me, but with my parents being so extremely social and sociable I knew no different and was always in their shadow. However they were wonderfully charitable and pro-active in so many ways that I was full of admiration for them – but who was I?

When I eventually took my O Levels I passed just one and a half subjects (the half being for special arithmetic, applicable to the Welsh examining board only), the other being music. Terrified of telling my father, his reaction was surprising – "one and a half more than I expected", he said. What was I to make of that? On my third attempt, and with my father's help in English Language, I managed to turn my previous two fails into an A pass and got enough O Levels to get me into a career in hospital administration, not altogether successfully, as I couldn't pass all the exams, but I did work as a clerk/ receptionist at the Cardiff Dental Hospital when it had just opened.

I was given the responsibility of setting up a colour-coded patient treatment system in the orthodontic clinic, whereby patient treatment could be seen at a glance by dentists and dental nurses alike. When I had started in the clinic, things were rather chaotic and it was satisfying to have set up a colour-coded system that worked, but there was no more challenge and challenge has, through my various evolutions, been a big motivator for me. So it was time for a change …

This was the "swinging 60s", and although I didn't swing too much in the way of festivals, drugs or *love-ins* I did hear the Beatles play live in Cardiff and also visited the Cavern Club in Liverpool with my cousin, who lived in the Wirral. I felt glad that I was an adolescent during this exciting musically shifting period, with the likes of Bob Dylan, Carol King, Joni Mitchell, Leonard Cohen and others that inspired my own singing with guitar accompaniment and song writing, which had started during this period.

During my late adolescence I had started to question my sexuality – not a subject that I wanted to share at home, and it made sense to me at this stage to go to a big city, where I could be anonymous and live more according to my inner world, which was, at this stage, only embryonic. This was not the period of openness that we find ourselves in today, topped by living in a small Jewish community, where the expectations were on me to marry, preferably to a nice Jewish boy. Some boyfriends at that time would have filled this requirement, but it was not where I was heading. But where was I heading? I did not know – I was a mystery unto myself, which enhanced feelings of isolation since I could not discuss this with anyone around me. It was my secret and I believed that there was something wrong with me, a belief that has haunted me on the path of "who am I?".

In not being able to embrace my sexuality fully I interpreted things wrongly, thinking that the opposite sex were not attracted to me, when, in fact, I was not attracted to the opposite sex. I believe my parents' only wish was for me to be married and have children and that this state represented success in life. A great deal of confusion played out in my inner world at this time, which I was wrestling with: what my parents' expectations were; and who I actually was? I had no idea, but embraced feelings of *failure* all around. A very grey world indeed.

As drama was one of the subjects that I had shown an aptitude for in school I thought I would become an actress and so I began to read *The Stage* magazine and looked at various options for theatre trainings. This was all carried out furtively and I kept copies under my bed, away from all eyes, or so I thought, but my brother had found a copy, and when I told him of my plans, he was supportive. I had set up an audition in Birmingham and all that was left to do was to tell my parents. This felt rather daunting, but I was strengthened by my cousin who had just become an art student in Bristol and had experienced the excitement of her settling in, which I'm sure gave me the confidence to go for it in my own life, to follow my heart, even though my heart didn't know itself. I wanted to find it …This marked the end of this decade and I found my parents quite surprisingly supportive of this journey into the *wilderness*.

Decade 3: Into the Wilderness

(1968/1978)

COMING OUT OF

Interestingly, as I stare at the blank page to begin to write about this decade I feel blank – very much how I must have felt as the 20-year-old me, about to embark on a very new experience. I was unaware, however, that I was so lost to myself at this stage of my life. I had moved away from home, at least, but my feelings were dead, devoid of excitement at this new life venture, a stranger to myself, ripe to take on roles as an actor (actress in those days), lost in my own wilderness. Not able to belong to myself; so who was I in facing the world of theatre students, relationships, "feeding myself", having fun?

I knew not, but I did not feel an outcast, since most students were claiming that they felt depressed – it seemed to be the acceptable *uniform* of the drama student, although I did not know I was depressed, at least   I was in a world where depression was acknowledged and even normalised, which felt comforting on one level. I was also making new friendships and taking acting roles that stretched me beyond my comfort zone. I was enjoying the chaotic mayhem of life at theatre school.

I took some strong leading roles in a sort of weekly repertoire training, to prepare us for the real world of theatre. The principal was a rather doubled-up old woman who I mistook for the cleaner when I first auditioned. The little theatre was so small that on one occasion a member of the audience fell out of the door and into the bushes, with most others in the audience evacuating the theatre to retrieve the casualty before the arrival of the ambulance – luckily none the worse for wear, which could not be said for the actors playing to an almost empty theatre.

The principal had a favourite repeated pep talk and it went something like this. Pity you can't hear me because I could mimic her voice very well:

"The world's going around 'duckie' and you've got to get on it when it's going around because it won't stop for you when it's going around because it goes round continuously. Now you know it and I know it, now stop it – that's theatre 'duckie'."

In my first few terms I was lodging with a family of four; the two children were repressed in the parent's presence and ran riot in their absence, and on one such an evening, while their parents were out, things got way out of control, and one fell through a glass door panel, which broke into smithereens. I was definitely out of there as soon as possible, but where?

Around this time I was approached by Mo, a female student at my theatre school, to share a room and flat with her, which I gratefully accepted. Interestingly, I spent every other weekend going back to Cardiff to stay with my parents and to receive some *spoiling*, as my mother would call it. My father, by this time, was a senior lecturer at the University of Wales in Cardiff, his subject being communication. With a sense of humour, and the subject of public speaking, as his particular specialist subject, he did a great many after dinner talks. I would often be taken along to these dinners with my mother and introduced as "my daughter, the actress", maybe enhancing the "seal of approval" I was always seeking from my mother. I rather enjoyed having a role to hide behind. On such weekends, I would be taken to the theatre, concerts and meals with my parents and wine and dine with their friends, and I think that made me feel rather special, but was also an effective screen to camouflage the *authentic* me, which was so confused.

On my 21st birthday, my parents arrived, unannounced, to my theatre school and parked their car unbeknownst to me in the car park opposite. One of my peers pointed to a car opposite madly beeping its horn, which seemed aimed at me, and it was. It was my parents proffering flowers and champagne, which was a lovely gesture; although how I jiggled my own arrangements around my parent's spontaneous visit was the question, and yet I felt very special having this much attention lavished on me.

Mo and I were on the top floor in an attic room and getting to know each other rather well – it was cosy. I would serenade her to sleep on my guitar, allowing the Bosa Nova rhythms of Stan Getz, to play out of my guitar and into her dreams. I felt as though I was very much in the protective role, perhaps projecting a part of myself that I'd never received; the song my mother never sang to me. We talked about art, poetry and film with an ease of communication I'd not experienced.

Sharing this same house was another female drama student called Jen, who I also developed an attachment to, and we often shared a bed together, enjoying feelings of physical closeness, both of us rather lost in our own worlds, like children holding hands for comfort in the night. I loved both, in my adolescent way, although neither of them knew this explicitly, I was much too afraid to share my intimate feelings.

This was not an altogether successful arrangement as Mo and Jen did not get on at all well and had an aversion to each other, so I was very much "piggy in the middle", going from one to the other, hoping to find something in my secret yearnings, through these relationships, which might redress the childhood losses of affection, caressing, soothing and comfort that I had so lacked.

I lived at different times with both these friends after my student days. I had a great deal of emotional attachment with both, which was more fantasy on my part than reality, but nevertheless held a great compulsive focus for my first forage into the world of relationships.

During this time I lived in London while being an out of work actress, auditioning for theatre work. As Mo and Jen were interested in exploring relationships with the opposite sex and I didn't seem to be so, it was rather a painful time.

While at Theatre School I joined up with four other theatre students to make a record – *Love Will Find A Way* with *Howard Walker and the Bombthrowers,* of who I was one, along with 3 other female students. We came to London to record it and stayed up all night in the process, which was a deal of fun at the time and getting to know London nightlife a little too. It has been captured on you Tube although I can't remember many sales at the time apart from my mother and myself but maybe it's an archive piece of its time and that's why it has been a record of its time – with seeds of the Beatles and a haunting heavenly refrain *Love Will Find A Way* https://youtu.be/qnUiRRYrpvg ripe for our present times while in Lockdown as the corona virus plays out its unpredictable attack on global structures and lives and racial riots break out in the US.

Halfway through my theatre school training, I auditioned for an acting job, as a way to get my Equity membership, which was difficult in those days and you needed to have the membership in order to get theatre and TV work. I was offered the part of Gretel in *Hansel and Gretel* and it was a tour with a Riverboat Theatre Company. There were seven in the company and we would split into two groups during the day, to perform to school children, and in the evenings, perform a review on the top of the boat, if the weather was good enough, or otherwise we would moor outside a pub and perform in the pub garden, if they had one, or in the pub if not.

It was a traditional hand-painted 70-foot narrow boat and we all lived on board, enjoying the lifestyle that living as "boatees" provided. It was a leisurely life on the Grand Union Canal that summer season, although since navigating the locks was not within my skills set, it meant running to join the boat at the next lock, providing exercise and the slimmest of waistlines I can ever remember having.

It was a tight fit on the boat and I shared the tiniest of cabins with another member of the cast. In order for one of us to have enough room to dress, the other had to disappear inside a cupboard. We all had chores to do on board the boat and were skippered by a traditional bargee, who could neither read nor write. As we had no written directions for our first night on board and could make no sense of directions such as "second lock after the butcher's shop", we failed to find the barge and had to spent the first night, instead of on the narrow boat, on the floor of my shared studio flat, all seven of us. One of the members of the cast was black, and wanting to be as politically correct as possible, we went overboard, not literally, in our attempts to welcome Clive in the name of equality, but he rejoiced in casting himself in the role of slave-master, since *he* paid *us* to carry out his chores on board the boat. We were grateful for a few extra pennies, as we were only earning around £11 a week, and we saw the humour in this reversal of roles.

It was romantic and claustrophobic living on board a narrow boat, but especially beautiful to see the countryside from the canal. I had never experienced the still silence and tranquillity of that pace of life, so quiet, away from the humdrum of the city. Schoolchildren would come to the boat to learn more about canal life, through drama improvisation, and became the work horses used to provide the horse power that engines eventually replaced.

On quiet evenings we would make our own entertainment and on one such an evening I was given the challenge of writing a song with some unpoetic words, such as aluminium, asbestos and nuclear, never thinking that some 50 years on I would be asked to sing it in Parliament as a message of foreboding about our climate crisis. The song is called "Once Upon A Child":

Once Upon A Child

Child can you see there's a metal tree
Standing alone in a field of stone
Leaves made of aluminium
Standing in isolation
Atomic germination
There

CHORUS

Was a time when there might have been
A Rock of Ages
Now it's made of plasticine

La la la la la la la
La la la la la la la

Child when you hear the first sounds of fear
Don't try to run from the concrete sun
This is the time for finding
Rainbows of polystyrene
Clouds with asbestos lining
There

CHORUS

Child when you feel there is nothing real
Look in the eyes of the old and wise
Could have been understanding
Thoughts of a larger landing
Wisdom and compromising
There

CHORUS

Other theatre tours and seasons were offered and gratefully accepted. This included a season at Swansea, being my first repertory season as an acting ASM (assistant stage manager) and then I was offered a children's tour with a theatre company in the Highlands of Scotland. Mo had also been offered a theatre job in Scotland and so it was possible to visit each other. I went to see her on one such an occasion only to find that she had fallen in love with a young scenic designer in the company and I was heart-broken. At the same time I also learnt that Jen was having a relationship with an ex-boyfriend of mine from my Swansea rep days. The betrayal I felt was excruciating as my fantasies were painfully falling apart and my sharing a little cottage with Mo or Jen were completely squashed.

The reality was that I was on my own, to face my life feeling lost and abandoned in the wilds of the beautiful Hebrides, not enjoying the lifestyle of being a touring actor at all, which included having to find different digs every couple of days in the depths of winter. I didn't enjoy the plays I was in or the theatrical company I was with, and I felt as if I was breaking down. In fact I now realise that I found that the social life involved in being in a theatre company went completely against the grain and this presented a huge challenge for me. So my personal, social and creative life was falling apart, as was my whole *false identity*. I would have succumbed to a nervous breakdown if I hadn't been so mortified at the thought of being visible as *not ok* to my parents and their friends, and so I just about held myself together, with thoughts of putting myself under an articulated lorry to get me out of the contract I was signed up to, as I didn't want to be blacklisted by Equity. No one knew how unhappy I was, apart from a few friends, but I was now returning to London, firmly convinced that I was out of theatre and alone, to live and find my way, quite stripped bare, but for once, *authentic*. How it hurt to have nothing to hide behind.

"The deeper that sorrow carves into your being, the more joy you can contain. Only when you are empty are you at standstill and balanced"
Kahlil Gibran, The Prophet

And so it was that I had to face the void of *what next*? I really had no qualifications, but had the gift of the gab, at least superficially. So I became a sales person. It provided a good income, and it also gave me flexibility to pursue singing studies, as I could finish my day around lunchtime, and as long as I did my calls I had no one breathing down my neck.

I was, however, struggling personally, as I was not developing relationships and wondered what was wrong with me. I became preoccupied with still being a virgin, as everyone else around me was experimenting sexually. I was lost and although I had some male encounters at this time, I was not bonding emotionally with the men in my life and my grey inner world was becoming darker.

It was with great relief the night I did lose my virginity, and less of a physical problem than I had thought. The man in question was a musician whom I had spent the afternoon with, composing and singing together, and it seemed important to me that he was emotionally unavailable, as I did not want to be exclusive and knew he had other relationships. Such was my low self worth.

posing and singing together, and it seemed important to me that he was emotionally unavailable, as I did not want to be exclusive and knew he had other relationships. Such was my low self worth.

In retrospect I believe now that my father had placed me on a pedestal and my emotional attachment to him was at the root of my *stuckness* in relationships. In fact, we had both put each other on pedestals that were unsustainable. If I was to move into my *authentic self* my father would have to come off his pedestal and in the living out of my cutting the umbilical cord our relationship sadly deteriorated.

During this period, I had some casual relationships with the opposite sex but without any serious intent but I was very glad, at least, to have lost my virginity. However I was not banking on ever having a serious relationship and the casual liaisons were risky and emphasised my lack of self-esteem.

Although acting was not intentionally on my agenda, I was offered some small TV acting roles, which I took on. One of them being a *Bride of Dracula* on the *Dave Allen Show*, (Dave Allen was an Irish comedian/satirist in the late 1960s to mid 1980s) where I made my entrance from a coffin – one of the few people to be alive **and** in a coffin.

I enjoyed TV in these circumstances as I could go home in the evening and avoid the sociability that I found so taxing in theatre. Around this time, I was offered an opportunity by an up-and-coming film director of the 1970s, to take part in some five-minute drama slots for TV, but I turned these down. I didn't feel confident enough to improvise with other actors, not knowing where and when my entrances and exits were, or what my lines would be. Who was I without a script? I, for sure, couldn't be an actress, as anyone in theatre would have given their right hand to work with Mike Leigh and the legend he became. So who was I if I wasn't an actor? The reason I gave for turning down the opportunity was that I was booked on a holiday to Nairobi, where I had been invited to stay with a friend in the theatre there. With no more thought of my lost opportunity,

I enjoyed an unforgettable holiday, making friends with the wildlife that matched my soul – the lions, hyenas, elephants, warthogs and a rather risky experience with a male DJ from my hotel in Mombasa, who wanted to show me more than the sights, which included his family, a nightclub (where being the only white woman was a threat to business for the black women) and finally a deserted, unlit house with 'some further wildlife expected', this could have led to a foursome, which frightened the life out of me and I refused to go in. The following morning I was on the beach taking a walk and I avoided the gaze of the hotel DJ, who was also taking a walk. "What's the matter? Have we had a divorce?" he asked. At least there didn't appear to be any hard feelings – and he had a good sense of humour.

And so it was I returned to London and the world of advertising, as well as a brand-new experience: I joined a Jewish choir. I enjoyed the dynamism of the social life, the interesting concerts in prestigious London venues and loved singing my heart out. We also travelled, participating in an International choir gathering in Israel, where I made some life-long friendships.

By this time the rent for my accommodation in London had escalated and it was my father who suggested that paying off a mortgage would be a better prospect than renting. This was a very good financial decision, which I certainly would not have had the practical sense to have prioritised. It has been an underlying stabilising factor in providing a sense of security for other projects that were to be my destiny in future decades. I have lived in my flat now for the past forty years and it has been my sanctuary.

Decade 4: Flowing

(1978/1988)

And so I sang my way into this new decade until fate would make my life take an uncanny turn. A friend, whom I had met in the choir, had put me forward to audition for a fringe theatre company, where, unbeknownst to me, the part that I was auditioning for would be a leading role.

This company had already established a reputation with Edinburgh fringe audiences as a comedy show where everything was doomed to go wrong. Edinburgh audiences loved this formula, so in getting back into theatre, albeit fringe, I experienced sold-out performances as audiences enjoyed a good belly laugh.

I took the role of the chairperson in these shows, within the setting of a Townswomen's Guild Dramatic Society, in which I played seven different parts, including that of a male solicitor. It was a musical tribute to Hollywood the first year I performed at Edinburgh and a murder mystery the second. The shows were physically very demanding and challenging dramatically, as the audience were part of the production, so it required some spontaneous improvisational patter from myself and other cast members. I enjoyed this very much, although I was stretched beyond my comfort zone. It provided the inspiration to propel me on to perform three one- woman shows in subsequent years, two of which I wrote myself.

Around this time, my brother got married and perhaps this precipitated my mother into urgently discussing my single status with my aunt. I, meanwhile, was involved with a post Edinburgh tour and on a Saturday night, after a theatre performance in York, which was fairly near where my aunt lived, it became apparent as events unfolded that a plot had been hatched to find me a man. Some deep discussions were held as to the type of man I would be interested in, I later found out, and it was deemed that I should fall into the arms of a Jewish delicatessen owner with an interest in theatre. My aunt said that she knew just such a man and a serious meeting was set up with his family and my aunt, to find out whether my family credentials could be matched with his. This was deemed to be so, and a dinner was set up in a restaurant in York.

It was a Saturday night and a busy one in touring theatre, as we had to strike the set after the show. This, however, failed to have any impact on the frantic tones of my mother's plea that I *had* to get there as soon as possible.

When I eventually arrived, I twigged what was going on immediately when I noticed the empty chair right next to this unknown man. I talked with him and we exchanged somewhat superficial conversation, with no chemistry between us whatsoever. As we were heading down the road out of the restaurant, my mother took me by the arm and said: "Well, what do you think?"I replied, thoughtfully, "I think he's gay." To which she replied, also thoughtfully and wistfully, that she did too. One wonders if that would have been ignored had I been at all interested?

In between my acting assignments, I was working as a sales person, which was conveniently flexible for my creative endeavours and it also brought me a good income. I had a good gift-of-the-gab (one of the positives I attribute to my mother, who could sell anything, even a car with a hole in the roof).

During this period I started to write my own one-woman shows based on my inner world, observations and thoughts, a stream of consciousness which often confused and amused audiences alike with their absurd overtones and undertones – much like life; complex and not altogether comprehensible.

BOBO REVEALS ALL

In one show I appeared with exposed plastic boobs (see above) giving an illustrated lecture about the meaning of life, looking beneath the superficial appearance of things, my plastic boobs; the central argument being to look for something more meaningful in life than the outer manifestation. In this case the false boobs, which were intended to show how ridiculous the idea of finding the meaning of life is, but it didn't stop me.

My father had illustrated this lecture and really captured my theories better than I could, with powerful illustrations. My concepts were probably, rather loosely rendered from the perspective of the Freudian connoisseur, in that context. In my interpretation the **gribenia**, a cloud of nastiness or depression needed to be attacked and exterminated by the **plunka**, the imagination.– My personal theory is very much a life statement that I hold to today after all the decades, albeit interpreted using my own vocabulary which I hope would have met with Freud's approval as our Austrian roots and generational influences might have acted as inspiration to both. My father recorded these performances, though these were poor quality, since the VHS video camera of the 1980s could not match the impeccable sound quality of our present-day versions.

It was after a performance at Wormwood Scrubs prison, to the *lifers*, which culminated in a near riot, that I had a revelation that I was more interested in these men's lives than I was in the performance aspect of my own one-woman shows. This was an inkling of a new dawning in my life, which did not manifest for a number of years but finally led me onto another path, which finally led to my becoming a psychotherapist some decades into the future.

As the prisoners were lined up ready to go back into their cells, I left Wormwood Scrubs with the scenery loaded on top of my car, feeling free of sorts, and yet my fascination with being imprisoned, as projected onto the *lifers*, seemed to kickstart something about the prisoner in me. After another Edinburgh run, I decided, finally, to give up theatre, as I had tested my creative boundaries to their limits and with it invested a considerable amount of money.

Although there is always some element of the actor in me, I had nowhere left to go but back to the drawing board. Not only did I give up theatre but threw all my toys out of the pram at the same time. I gave up my sales job also. I think I was determined to find a more *authentic* pathway for myself, whatever and wherever that might be.

Around this time, I learnt that my father had been diagnosed with cancer, which was deemed terminal. It was a quick decline, and to be a catalyst in my re-establishing moments of real connection with him as I sat at his bedside, just simply being with him, holding his hand, and in this simple act maybe my father received what he'd never had in life; an understanding female presence.

In one such moment, he was insistent that he wanted to get out of the bed and lie on the floor. It seemed so important for him to do so that I enabled him to roll out of the bed, my body taking his weight, and letting him fall softly to the floor, which put him in a state of ecstasy, no doubt the morphine talking, but I felt glad to have had this moment with him and it was worth everything to have done so. However when the GP arrived she was furious that I had allowed this to happen as it was near impossible to put him back into bed.

In contrast, my mother could not take the painful reality of his decline on board and her way of dealing with it was to keep busy, trying to keep normal routines going, which included doing crossword puzzles, listening to loud TV quiz programmes and demanding participation from my father as he looked helplessly on.

And so the death of my father marks the end of my fourth decade. I wrote this poem as a tribute to the ebb and flow of my relationship with him and it was written many decades after his death.

DAFFODILS IN THE MIRROR

Coughing Man

Open skies grey with unshed rain

Yellow fields, ploughed tracks leading around bushes.

Man coughing and coughing

irritation hitting, biting forth onto the day.

Open landscape to

Heaven knows what on my way to retreat.

Cows stand

meadow banks enclose and comfort

like the moon sign says "sleep walk".

Coughing, coughing again

the man sips water

sharing a table on the train.

Hay stacks neaten my irritation

Hedgerows grow my tolerance.

Maybe it's cancer like my father's – cough, cough,

coughing until he died.

No diagnosis, no diagnosis.

Memories unfold as to this path

in a complicated relationship.

It was hard, it was fun it was mad it was bad

it was love it was hate it was stifling

It was love it was hate it was stifling

It was love it was hate ......It was

love.

Decade 5: Growing

(1988/1998)

THE LOST VISCOUNTESS

In the wake of my father's passing, I was concerned about my mother, as the carers thought that she might fall apart in the wake of so much denial, but with many friends around her and her own strength of character, although visibly fragile, her life continued.

I was surprised at how resilient she was, and on one occasion, when she was called upon to make a speech at a public-speaking competition in my father's name, she triumphed in sharing a heartfelt speech, note-free, to the young up-and-coming award winners and I understood, on reflection, that the public performance side of my life was just as prominent on my mother's side as it had been on my father's.

This was a difficult time, however, as I lived in London and it seemed a long emotional distance to Cardiff at the time, but my mother and I did spend many holidays together and I was glad to travel with her to stay with relatives in Florida and Israel, on the Nile at Luxor, and in Prague, Paris and other such destinations. Although an *authentic* connection was difficult, I enjoyed these times.

Around this period I joined a women's writing group and it was there that I was to encounter a life-changing relationship with a French-Italian woman that lasted on and off for some thirty years.

Sabine was an aristocrat, brought up in the bohemian Paris of the 1950s, with some of the literary feminists and surrealist legends of that time, whom she had personally known. These included the likes of Simone de Beauvoir, Violet Leduc, Andre Breton and Jean Cocteau. I was caught up in a Parisian culture bubble and I found something stylish and exotic in her, while ignoring her spontaneous outbursts and observations, which at first seemed quite refreshing, but which in time I realised could cause chaos; she was the antithesis of my adaptive False Self.

While I tried so hard to fit into the discipline of the school system, she boasted with glee about how she had been expelled from an assortment of Catholic boarding schools for disruptive behaviour, which had included supposedly *sinful* relationships with other girls.

This was a marriage made in heaven to the "nice misplaced Jewish girl" who did not seem to fit in anywhere. Sabine was outspoken about her sexuality and fresh out of a divorce. She was physically available even if emotionally she was not. Sabine, in the role of *aristocrat*, acted as if she had been pardoned from the real world and lived in a position of heightened *superiority*.

On numerous car journeys to visit various beautiful parts of the UK, she would lie on the back seat looking out at the sky as I chauffeured her on our many journeys together. I was not used to expressing myself in relationships and went along with the role that I found myself in. Also she showed an interest in my creative endeavours, which was an important aspect to our relationship. I was smitten. We got together around the time of my father's death and also, quite by coincidence, the death of her brother, who died on the same day as my father. It was a much more enticing option to travel and get to know each other than to deal with the grieving process. I saw parts of Britain that I would never have discovered; so informed was she on places of beauty and culture and art that had been sadly lacking in my own life. And so a part of the *authentic me* was beginning to be sculpted into life; more, in fact, than I ever could have imagined.

She was not one for deep concentration; more for capturing moments of beauty in her garden, and on one such day she got out her pastels and in the effortlessness of the moment, and the lack of expectation of any end result, her spontaneity was contagious, and so I started expressing myself by trying to put on paper how I felt rather than trying to capture the precision of what I saw.

SABINE IN HER GARDEN

I enjoyed the experience of making marks with no exact goal apart from the enjoyment of the moment. Art had been so beyond my reach at school that making marks of colour from a pleasurable stance, without expectation, was an intoxicating cocktail; all the more so for the fact that no one was judging me; the doing of it was the liberation. And so the *painter* in me was born and my grey inner world was fast turning to colour.

Not content with the odd garden moment I went to all different sorts of art classes, immersing myself into all that I could, with the feverish passion of unleashed energy. At home I would copy Matisse and Picasso, where obvious inaccuracies actually interested me, as I felt my way into my own style without a clue as to what I was actually doing.

Others were impacted by my spontaneous expression and thought: if she can do it, so will I and so I ran some creative art workshops at the same time as I was teaching myself and they were a joyful experience for others as well. Nothing in my life before had ever been able to flow as it did at this time. I felt like a lion let out of its cage at long last, and I could finally connect with all the parts of myself. I was growing but I could not make any sense out of it all except that it was happening, I could not find the words…

At this time I was employed in another sales job – selling stand space for exhibitions in London and the Midlands and doing very well, with a company car provided, but I was not happy and It was during this period that I went on an art holiday to the South of France, staying in a little hamlet outside Apt in the Luberon region. As there was no room for me in the main house Ifound myself in the villa opposite, staying with my hostess Isabelle, who happened to be the village healer, using sound as her means of healing.

She and I were not proficient in each other's language but that did not stop us from making ourselves understood. I had my guitar with me and was writing songs; she had assumed that I was a singer, not a sales rep. I was pretty depressed while there, without quite knowing why.

Sabine came to join us in the second week and with her fluent French real language communication became possible. In a gesture of trust Isabelle, who was leaving to go to Paris to see her daughter, offered us her house and car so that we could explore the region.

Some years later she came to visit Sabine and I in London, and while showing her parts of North London, I also showed her some photos of myself at my work Christmas party, all in festive spirit. She freaked out and said that I had to get out of the place, it was stifling me, and I should be singing – that was what I was meant to do.

After she left and I was resting on the bed recovering from such an intense experience and within the silence of relaxation I heard the most beautiful bell-like sound, such as I have never heard, or that I could describe in any rational way. I sensed that she had reached the *authentic* part of myself and the truth was ringing out and ringing in. So with no practical thought in mind I gave my notice in on the following Monday and said goodbye to my company car and my work colleagues.

How on earth I would manage financially was a huge concern. I just leapt into that abyss. As fate would have it an aunt of mine died in America around that time and left me enough money to buy a good second-hand car. I prayed for clarity as to how to proceed further on my path. What manifested was a whole new career as a singer-guitarist in residential homes for the elderly, nursing homes and hospitals – in fact anywhere where people were unable to get out into the world and I could bring the world to them with a programme called *Around the World in Music*.

I acted as my own agent, sales being so much a part of my background, and I had enough time to follow my journey pursuing art studies. I had been interested in doing a certificate course in arts and therapy and was awarded a bursary from Equity, the actors' union, to do so, but I really felt that I would like to put that bursary to my art studies instead and it was agreed that this could happen, provided I went to a well established art college. So I ended up at The Slade School of Fine Art, part-time, where I had free choice to select courses that interested me up to the bursary value. There I gained some confidence, as I was encouraged to follow what was my specific interest and go for it obsessively.

A WHOLE NEW CAREER AS SINGER/GUITARIST

I was also interested in sculpting and in one session we were given the instructions to make an armature on which to sculpt a small head in red wax while looking at the model. The exercise required us to rotate the wheel and look and sculpt the head from the various different angles. I looked around at others in the class and felt that I had not understood – I seemed to be doing things differently and so I ripped my head apart and started again. In the break the tutor came to me and asked why I had done what I did and I replied, "Well, I got it wrong" and he responded, "You were the one that got it right". That was a big learning curve for me as I could never trust that I had understood instructions correctly in a learning group, and always looked to others for validation that I *had* got it right. Being seen as being right in this respect against the group was deeply therapeutic for me as I learnt to trust myself and my instincts. I remember sitting outside The Slade building in the grounds of the University of London, feeling so deeply connected and in such a beautiful setting, both architecturally and educationally. I felt

ABSTRACT LION

that I belonged at long last. I was growing. Had my father ever thought of me in such a way, I think he would have been proud.

While at The Slade I heard of some studios for rent in the Chocolate Factory in Wood Green and so I invested in one, way before I could really afford it or knew what I was doing and I have been there ever since, growing into myself through painting. I began to exhibit and sell in a way that I could never have imagined; my paintings were exhibited in Dallas and Paris, with solo exhibitions in London and Cardiff. I was offered an artist's residency in an art centre in Cambridgeshire which I had to turn down because life's events unfolded in an unexpected way.

At the time of my second exhibition, which my mother had attended, she discovered a bruise on her shin that was not healing and after many x-rays, she was diagnosed with cancer of the bone, deemed to be terminal, with no available treatment. My career ground to a halt as I returned to Cardiff. My mother displayed tremendous strength and courage, not showing any evidence that she had processed the news. Because of her courage and visible fragility she attracted loving feelings from all around her, thereby dissolving the screen that had rebuffed love, care and affection that she so genuinely hungered for. It was easier to love her while she was so vulnerable. However driving her car was another matter; she still had to be in the driving seat, right until the very end, and her friends asked why I wasn't doing the driving. I couldn't answer because it was a compulsive need for her to retain a semblance of control. There was also a regular team of home carers that provided 24-hour nursing care, until such a time that she went into a hospice in Penarth, one of her favourite places. This was also one of the most beautiful locations for a hospice, overlooking the sea, where she could also still have the ice cream she so loved from Rabbioti's – always such a special treat for her.

I was pleased to be able to show my love and affection at this time in a way I had never been able to do while she was healthy. My brother and I were there for her last conscious breath as she went into a coma and slowly died, comforted that we were both by her side.

Decade 6: Belonging

(1998 / 2010)

This decade starts with my connecting to feelings I had never experienced before; I had never been in my life without my mother and without my "protective shield" of dissociation that had been my particular defence mechanism, giving me some false feelings of strength.

In retrospect this was also how my mother must have learnt to survive in her life, devoid of painful emotions. This was the result of what she lacked from her own mother, which in turn was passed onto me, within the realm of what is now referred to as, or what cannot be talked about.

In the painting "Two in One" I wonder now, as the therapist, at the connection of the two female shapes as they blend into each other. Who is who *(see page 56)*? A shape is escaping into the light … perhaps it is the part of me that has not been killed off.

The maternal bond, I hazard a guess, had never been experienced enough within my female heritage to deal with much more than material and practical survival, which was success of itself. And in the wake of that I experienced an *absence* where "a maternal physical bond" had not been felt. I learnt a "survival at all costs" strategy, developing a False Self survival mechanism at a very young age, where I was valued for being obedient and adaptive, and I believed that if I hid my emotions and tamed my individuality and spontaneity, pretending my vulnerability did not exist, then that was success indeed. A protective defence which also dismantled any sense of authenticity and how damaging that is. At the same time I gained the inspiration to go searching for my *authentic* self.

This energy in my body, in the wake of my mother's passing, I felt viscerally, like a stabbing white light into my heart; a sheet of glass penetrating an overwhelming sense of space, in a torrent of extreme and unprocessed feelings.

Going into the studio and closing the door on the world was the only way I could cope, by painting and painting and painting.

The sheer release of my primitive feelings through paint, texture and colour was unstoppable and I found that even the critical and negative voices that were my constant companions during my lifetime and through this intense period of my life could not stop me. I was sitting in my own light at long last. The symbolic black bird in the image of "Baby in a Bottle" in Decade One is now white, a dove-like bird calling me to climb the ladder.

I now realise that these critical and negative voices were in part what I had inherited from my mother, for when others spoke positively about my paintings, my mother was still unable to find it within herself to do so; praise was foreign in my world. So while the

IN MY OWN LIGHT

world was welcoming my paintings, my mother could not. Still critical, she would add her comments, "Too busy" or "Too blue", "Looks like an old boot" to my abstract vision of a face.

In the wake of her comments I could see why I had such a lack of confidence and I started to change my own critical voice within so that when I felt I had made a mistake on my canvas I just put more energy into that part of my painting and learnt that it would become something more than I could ever have imagined, creating an interesting dynamic that could alter the whole painting.

I was learning to go with the flow and trust that all was not lost by making a mistake; probably the biggest lesson I have ever learnt. I could now see how my False Self was formulated from the belief that I thought that every part of my True Self was a mistake and everything *authentic* about me should be changed.

Needless to say, this very painful state of affairs leads to mental distress. In understanding more about recovery from "narcissistic abuse", or you could say "unconscious toxic parenting". In my case my parents were always physically present, so there was no explicit evidence of parental abandonment, but emotionally I experienced them as absent. This emotional absence makes sense now as my parents lacked good role models in their own upbringings. I felt my role in childhood was to meet

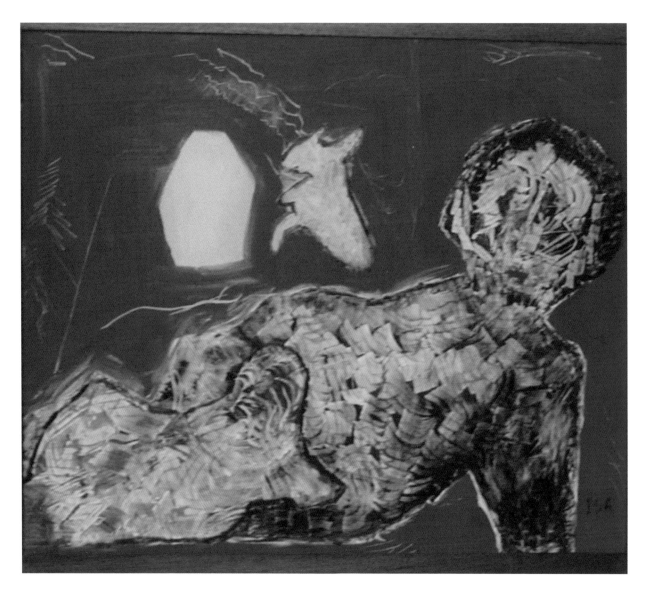

TWO IN ONE

their needs rather than my own. The child tries to please the parent, as a natural human adaptation, and in my case my True Self disappeared and became invisible through what is sometimes referred to as *dissociation*, the natural human survival mechanism when there is too much strain and stress for the child and so the child becomes disembodied within the state of *dissociation*. The major characteristic of all dissociative phenomena involves a detachment from reality.

In psychology, **dissociation** is a wide range of experiences, from the low and very human mild detachment when we dislike an experience and pretend it's not happening, to more extreme and severe detachment from physical and emotional experiences. Dissociation is commonly displayed on a continuum.] Some years prior to my mother's

COLOUR OF SORROW

death I had joined a Buddhist group. I could see that it was very human to have negative mind chatter and to accept and challenge this is the art of *mindfulness*. I was glad to be part of a community and not alone in my inner world vulnerability. I felt privileged to have monks and nuns teaching me about reality; that is the ability to stay present with *what is* rather than escape. These people radiated a sense of presence; their stillness and compassionate humour for our very human condition of *mindlessness* was a great innovating motivator for me to learn gentleness and compassion in relation to the harsh, critical and judgemental voices that were not only a personal legacy I came to understand, but also very human. So I wasn't alone and others suffered in the same way as I had. It was a relief to know that I was a human being after all, rather than an *alien*, which I often felt.

MOTHER IN MY FLAT

SAILING

During this period I lost over seven stone by taking meal replacements over an 18-month period but sadly only to regain the weight over a further 18 months. This is a personal area of my life that I am still addressing as *unfinished*.

Many paintings flowed and I just showed up every day at my studio, sometimes facing the blank canvas or sometimes continuing on a painting that I had started previously, approaching it with new eyes. Sometimes I would learn in classes, but I was opening to my *authentic self* and allowing the unknown to pour out. I was beginning to sell paintings also, which left me speechless in the wake of creating something that people actually liked before I really knew what I was doing. **They** bought and **I** painted: assortments of flowers, landscapes, portraits and abstracts and I was alive – very.

Each day I would express on a canvas events happening in the external world or my internal one: I was learning just how much energy is trapped within our negative self-judgments as I danced out my paintings.

At this same time I set up creative arts workshops for children and adults alike, facilitating a safe and non-judgemental space for others' self-expression and found that the images they were creating flowed from the participants also, connecting to parts of themselves that had long been killed off in the efforts to fit into our supposedly civilised society. But just how civilised is it?

Our society is, by its own hands, falling apart. We lose our souls within the confines of an educational system with the bias towards ticking more and more boxes. As evidence of someone who failed miserably in the academic system, I fear we have a long way to go. I think our world could be more switched on if our educational system included encouragement for the unique gifts of its young ones. In addition to learning to adapt to the world of exams at ever-younger ages, thereby passing judgments of success or failure on a child so early in life. Does passing exams and high achieving make a good human being? Surely not.

My own therapeutic practice shows me that high achievement can often be an outward cover for those who are inwardly depressed, anxious and narcissistically wounded. The speed of the world and systems of heartless communications within organisations might create the societal camouflage of *success* – but creates a real disconnect from the mind, heart and spirit. We only have to look at the increasing male suicide rate of students in the UK, who sadly take their own lives and do not share their unique offerings and capabilities with this world; and young girls needing to create the *perfect* bodies as seen on social media including a genital uniformity enhanced by plastic surgery and a real disconnection from reality – an escape into the perfect body that can never be…

During the period after my mother's passing, I experienced a chance encounter. I had been to a book launch at the Ladies' Pond in Hampstead, and went to a local café to cool down on a hot summer's day with a friend. All the seats at the outside tables were packed as it was so hot, all but two, that is, and we sat opposite a couple. The man was quite chatty and before long I was showing him an art magazine, where I had been awarded a prize of £100 of art materials and given the title "artist of the month", for my seascape pastel painting of "Birling Gap". The next thing I knew, I was showing him my little portfolio album of photos of paintings and he stopped at a photo of a tree that I had painted in my local park, Waterlow, in Highgate. He asked me where that painting was and I said "in my studio" and he said – "Ok – I'd like to buy it. Let's go there now". So, always up for a potential sale, I said goodbye to my friend and climbed into his car, stunned that anyone would offer to buy a painting without even seeing it in its true glory, or at least haggling over the price. Buying a painting, unlike purchasing a fridge or a

INTO THE NEW MILLENNIUM

washing machine, is normally a process approached cautiously by the purchaser, I've noticed. What will my friends and family think of me? Am I marked for life? A fridge or washing machine can be replaced in five or six years, but what of a painting? What will happen to it after my death?

While we were driving through Alexandra Palace, with the beautiful views of London to our right, he told me that he was a fourth-generation Quaker and a publisher, and if he was to buy my painting I should buy his latest Quaker publication *Silence of the Word*. I

CONCEPTION

hastily agreed. £2.50 seemed a fair exchange. However, knowing that he was a Quaker somehow relaxed me. I never saw him again, but what followed was exciting.

When we got to the studio, I think it's fair to say that there was bedlam as shelves were ran sacked to see all my wares, and it was a feverish hour or so. In the end, he did not buy the tree painting but two others to the same value. Deed accomplished the only thing unaccounted for   was the payment, and so I had to stick with the couple until the final transaction had been completed – the paintings were now wrapped up and in the boot of his car. Luckily I didn't have any plans for the evening, as on my way into the supermarket, where he hoped to get some cash, he invited me to join them for dinner, which I agreed to do.   I felt, somehow, that this man was really living his life spontaneously and going with the flow, as was I, and we all enjoyed a great evening together in a house where he was staying for the weekend, surrounded by original paintings by Sir Stanley Spencer. I ended up playing my guitar and singing and really sharing from my heart.

When I read his pamphlet *Silence of the Word* it resonated. I had found no words since my mother's death to express my feelings, as my paintings had been my words. There was a link here somewhere, I believed, but I did not gain this information from my logical mind; more from a deep place within.

So I decided to go to my first Quaker meeting in August 1998 after having read my new friend's pamphlet and I have been going ever since. The silent meeting for worship

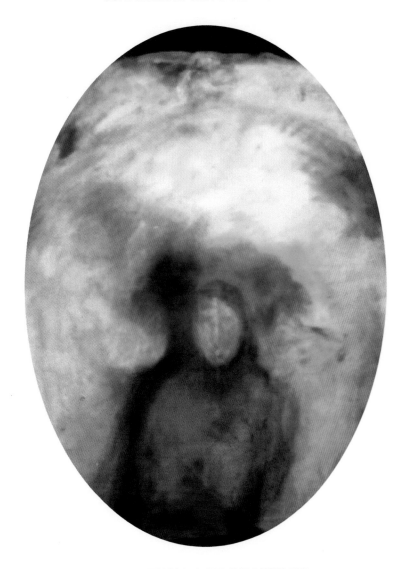

IN MY PRISM: A SELF-PORTRAIT

appealed, as did the Quaker principle of "that of God within". It has, however, taken some years for me to become aware that my "True or Authentic Self" – "that of God within"– is a meeting place for my personal, spiritual, creative and therapeutic self to unite, somewhere deeper than the ego and where, eventually, freedom can be found.

"In My Prism: A Self-Portrait" was painted after I had had a photograph taken of my colour aura at a mind, body spirit festival. I was intrigued to know whether the colours would change if I had other readings marking different moods, events and life's circumstances – as yet on my to do list.

As I was coming to terms with the death of my mother and four other women also, some of them my own age, I was questioning how one could celebrate life while at the same

FEMALE RESURRECTION

time experiencing a plethora of females around me dying; maybe a part of me was dying also. And so, with this in mind, I decided to put the female on the cross.

I think I was also marking a spiritual crossover in my life that linked many aspects of my *Authentic Self* that lay beyond words. This created tremendous guilt for me as I felt a traitor to my own cultural heritage – and that I was betraying my roots by putting myself, like Jesus, on the cross. And, as if that wasn't upsetting enough for me, in my research on the symbol of the cross, I found that the Aramaic root of Jesus is my name, Isa.

Oh my God !!!!!!

I had a vague idea that there would be three female figures but allowed the painting to paint itself, if you like. What my original concept did not envisage was that the central figure would transcend while I was in the process of painting her. Her head was nowhere to be seen: off the canvas. This was a miracle indeed. And so I called the painting the "Female Resurrection", a transcendent image of suffering and transformation.

I had inherited a very large blank canvas at the time (7' x 5.5') and had always wanted to work on a canvas that big, this was my opportunity. With the concept of the central

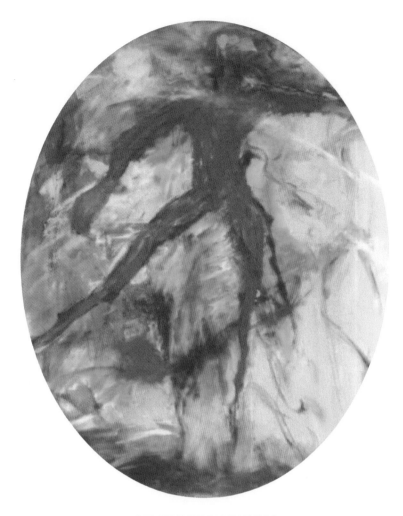

CELEBRATION IN PINK

female figure being outstretched with her arms seven feet across, I would put two other female figures on either side like a crucifixion scene. The figure on the left, looking into a sort of conch, was the face of reflection and the other, on the right of the painting, a dark figure wearing the crown of thorns, but decidedly dancing into the painting. Around 2002 or 2003 I exhibited in some five solo exhibitions and sold many paintings – it was a very exciting time after having produced some 450 art works, but I was realising that the intensity of my journey was fast failing me and I had nowhere else to go but to close my studio door and open the door onto the world. I had learnt so much about myself from this personal and spiritual experience that I wanted to share it, but I did not know how. I could not put any of this into words but just followed my spirit, as I had done in the past and trusted that all would be fulfilled in the fullness of time.

I found myself becoming aware of an unopened door from an earlier period in my life. The certificate course in arts and therapy that I had almost participated in some ten

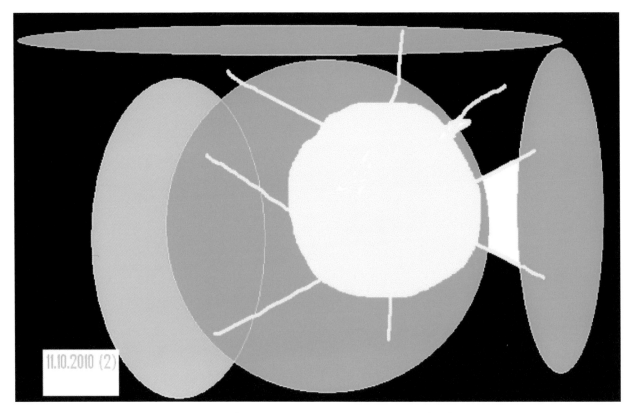

EXISTING IN THE VOID OCTOBER 11TH, 2010

years before; it had now become a diploma and masters course which was four years part-time. I didn't know how I would fare on such a journey, but I was interested to make sense of my extraordinary creative and spiritual life experiences and thought the course might fill some gaping holes in my personal life (the blank canvas). However, without an A Level to my name, facing a masters course was more than daunting at the age of 55. The dean assured me that if I could tick the boxes of prior accredited learning, I could apply to do it and so it was. I was granted a place on this masters course, a complete novice to academia.

I failed my first essay, as I failed another five assessments. I remember doing my first case presentation as a performance, thinking that I should get a round of applause at the end of it. Instead of this there was a deathly silence and the examiner asked me what my thinking was, to which I had none. She pulled me aside afterwards and said I looked like a rabbit caught in the headlights. I realised that my approach to things was instinctive and if I was to get through this course, I would have to learn about structure, evidence, making an academic argument around comparative theories; all very scary untapped organisational formations that were yet to be found within my humble, as yet virginal, but curious mind.

Many people veer towards the more structured, organised part of the brain, so-called left-brain function and I more towards the right-brain function: instinctive, creative, abstract. My peers, mainly much younger than I, and high achievers, in the main, could not fathom out how I could carry on with my studies with so many failures to my credit. I was working through my academic demons which were rife from the past and reassured myself that as I was being partly funded by Equity and that of a Quaker charity for mature students, I could not pay back the huge fees, but I think, more importantly, I was learning on the job.

On failing my second clinical exam for being too eclectic, I was very near failing overall and another clinical exam failure would mean that I would be off the MA. I was in serious trouble and decided to reach out to the dean, who had called me aside some time before, as being an 'enigma' to him. He wanted more visibility from me and asked me how likely it would be for me to ask for help if I needed it, on a scale from 0/10. I said 6. He said he thought that was a bit high and I felt the tears well up.

Now was the time to reach out and I did. Had I not had this earlier meeting with him I might have remained totally lost in my world of *failure*. What did I need to do to get through the course? I was stumped. Two hours went by in the large orange rococo room, where I met with the dean and the head of studies, drank numerous cups of tea and wrestled with the confusion of what was required of me to get through this course. Some sort of clarity emerged whereby they wanted more visibility from me. What were my particular standpoints and theoretical underpinnings? Be compulsive, I was told. Go to conferences in the areas of your specialised interests, which in my own case was an inspiration, as I was motivated by areas of my deepest wounding, in the area of early maternal neglect and the impact of that on attachment throughout life and the belonging or not belonging to Self in relation to that absence. I felt very contained within these parameters and more grounded as to how to proceed.

In my final viva presentation, and not without a blip beyond my control caused by the examiners, who had to leave the room, I passed with a distinction and finally got my masters with an overall *merit*, so I was now a MAM; MA with Merit.

Wow is all I can say to that…

Until the day I received
my Masters:
It's a Pass 11.10.2010

HAUNTED HOUSE

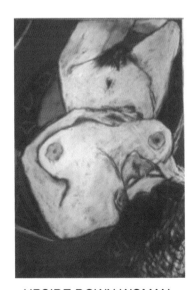

UPSIDE DOWN WOMAN

SEA OF HOPE

CAPE CORNWALL

Of Paintings

BRIDE AND GROOM

THINKING WOMAN   MONTSEGUR   MAN WITH RED TURBAN

MEMORY TO MY ROOTS: AFTER KITAJ

I identify as a Jew ancestrally, culturally and creatively through my Eastern European roots; in particular the Eastern European artists of the early and mid-twentieth century. I identify as a *survivor* of the intergenerational trauma that links me to my personal heritage; in the grandparents I never knew, my parents who loved in the wake of their unexpressed traumas and all the *victims* of abusive regimes of power where the lessons of the Holocaust remain unlearnt.

I identify as a Jew belonging to a family of "not belonging" – I remain a "wandering Jew" to any label that restricts personal journeying and discovery that could upset the status quo of a fundamentalist and rigid system of control whether it be religious, spiritual, racial, familial, relational or political.

SHOSHI RAYNER

RABBI'S DAUGHTER

Decade 7: Speaking from the Heart

(2008/2018)

The beginning of this next decade sees me sporting my cap and gown and attending my graduation ceremony; a miracle indeed. I had never consciously thought about a career as a psychotherapist, because as far as I was concerned, I was doing an MA in *me*, trying to fill in the gaps where I had become lost; reclaiming and understanding how I had become lost, and in so doing, find some answers.

However, now 11 years into my psychotherapeutic practice I find that it has been a fascinating and illuminating experience, which carries me through my work with clients; for the identity problems I had experienced are very much what most clients I see have also suffered. More than that, I am also mindful, to a greater or lesser degree, that it's part of the human condition to wrestle with the demands of being human, which requires our vulnerability as being a strength rather than a weakness; keeping our struggles out of reach is the real problem, for when we dare to have the courage to look closely at our inner world we can begin to heal and redress falsities that have produced distorted thinking and beliefs.

When we have lived through and survived early parental neglect through unconscious narcissistic abuse, the damage we feel in adulthood is difficult to locate. The child might have had all material and practical needs met, but still feel empty and desolate as an adult, as needs for spontaneous expression have been suppressed to adapt to the family environment, and in so doing lose a significant part of the True Self. So loss and isolation become loud in the adult's inner world as the unique life-force has been murdered and cries out to find a voice. Instead of the parent meeting the child's developmental needs for mirroring in order for them to develop a natural sense of Self, the child's True Self withers as the False Self grows.

Like animals, we humans have basic needs to be loved, stroked, taken care of and reassured and soothed when feeling troubled, by being physically close to the mother when we are children. If the mother, parent or primary care-giver, for whatever reason, is not able to meet the child's basic needs in this respect, the child learns to adapt to a false set of conditions that bypass the basic human needs. For example, if they are asked to "Be silent, be good, be brave, don't cry", the child interprets a "You're not special enough to be loved" inner voice, which is contrary to their natural needs and so the inner child grows up out of sorts; outwardly appearing grown up but inwardly traumatised and unable to meet life's challenges head-on, without some sort of mental torment, since meeting the new as a necessary developmental stage has never

SELF PORTRAIT

happened. The script from this False Self is that to be invisible and hide is the name of the game, the *success*, and all the gifts and richness that make up the True Self remain hidden in a deeply held core belt of shame.

In working with clients, my sense of drama plays a large part in my work as an arts psychotherapist and once a trusting relationship has been established, I let humour and "larger- than-life" dramatisations of the unlived parts of the client's life begin to live again as they can step into the gaps in their lives more readily. A stage has been created within which the True Self can exist at long last and therefore a truer picture can be painted.

The stage is set in which the damaging impact of the "false, critical, controlling and neglectful self", which becomes internalised, can at last be seen for what it is and the process of mindfully dismantling these false beliefs can be activated. Once the client can start to see these different parts playing out inside themselves, they can learn to adopt a more observant part of themselves in order to change the "critical and negative voices" and foster an altogether more nurturing and compassionate tone. This is far from being easy work, but the "lost child within the adult" can become alive again – free and liberated, much as I learnt to do through my painting process.

I find, while working with clients, that I am in the flow of life. This is facilitating a space for others to become more aware of themselves in the present and so enable the possibility of positive change and transformation within my clients' lives. This being in the *now* also connects to my Buddhist practice of *mindfulness*, and the Quaker reference to "that of God in everyone" – space for a truthful heartfelt connection within oneself.

While I was studying for my MA, I was invited to exhibit in a solo exhibition at the Ben Uri Gallery in London. The paintings I exhibited were very much along my *authentic* journey of becoming my True Self and the exhibition was entitled *My Journey into Belonging*. I had wanted to exhibit my "Female Resurrection" picture but it was too large to get down the small and winding staircase. I was pleased to see, however, that the gallery did have an excellent exhibition on the subject of the cross as a symbolic metaphor. Alongside the obvious Christian significance, I rejoiced in this exhibition, looking at the cross from differing artists' perspectives, as I had suffered such a profound anguish in the process of painting the "Female Resurrection" and my need to put myself as a Jewish female on the cross, which triggered a sense of guilt and betrayal to my religious and cultural heritage.

Some four or five years on I had a more abstract painting exhibited at La Galleria in Pall Mall as a finalist in the East/West Arts Awards and also exhibited in the Crypt Gallery in St. Martin in the Fields, Trafalgar Square, with two other female Quaker artists – one with a Christian background, one with a Hindu background and myself being Jewish. Together we explored how our past cultures had influenced our work; the exhibition was called "Inside Out; Outside In" – a series of internal and external human landscapes.

In the midst of this exhibition I endured some serious pain in my left hip and a few months later I had a hip replacement surgery followed by the same on my right hip some weeks later. Since then my mobility has not been up to par but I am mobile enough and glad to be without the pain I suffered prior to the hip replacements.

I am now approaching my seventieth birthday and with much personal reflection and a resistance to celebrate this coming of another age, a stream of feelings is flooding through me and some of them are very unpleasant indeed. Timewise 70 is a ripe number of years to live on this earth as a human being and yet if I stand beside a ripe old oak tree I feel that all that has been my life so far is so very young and in many ways I am touching my immature feelings that had to be hidden as the one-year-old who learnt not to cry and missed out on so much necessary early development that might

CLIMBING THE MOUNTAIN

have led to my becoming an *adult* prior to my seventieth year. The wall that protected my heart from exposure, in order to protect my *True Self*, is falling now and revealing feelings of a volcanic nature, such that I never thought I possessed behind my protective screen – me intolerant? Never! Impatient? Can't be me! I understand now that these impatient feelings were not permissible in my younger life, and so it is not surprising that they rise with all their vengeance, wanting to destroy the very lifeforce that is my *authentic self* as I finally come out of hiding.

"The heart is never tarnished or touched; it is the sea of the soul. It is the mind that leads us astray. Peace, bliss, happiness and grace are the qualities of the heart. By tuning into the 'feelings of the heart' you are able to experience your natural innocence, that innocence you had as a child."

Maitreya's Teachings
The Laws of Life Edited by Benjamin Creme, 2005

So today I feel my nakedness, stripped bare of all but my pulse's rhythm, my heart's beat and my breath's sigh and I do exist without having to prove myself. I am enough, I am, and knowing that this time of transition into another decade is the natural path of evolution, which includes my resistance.

My inner beast is meeting the "beast from the East" – it is March 2018. Snow and below zero temperatures appear for their second penetrating March visit, as if to hold me by the hand with its reminder of the coldness that I have endured on this lifetime journey, where my emotions were screened off and my False Self want to prompt me that: "I don't deserve to be loved", which is harsh for the *lost child*. The escape I succumbed to in order to deal with those feelings was comfort eating. This voice can continue in a downward spiral on a bad day and get played out in a melodramatic way in the power of negative self-chatter. I now understand that unpleasant feelings that go with it are exactly as they're meant to be, even though I am now aware that I was the one rejecting myself. I do not have to pretend or prove myself any more as I now belong to myself. Having "peace of mind" is freedom. I now allow my difficult feelings to exist within, as Eckhart Tolle says in the *The Power of Now*:

"An emotion has a very short life span. It is like a momentary ripple or wave on the surface of your Being. When you are not in your body...an emotion can survive inside you for days..."

And I would add *or* a lifetime, unless understood through self-knowledge and a compassionate self-acceptance. This is not an easy journey as M. Scott-Peck writes in his book *The Road Less Travelled* about the therapeutic journey.

Our authentic path is unique and no one else can know what our inner world dictates. Some of us grow and change within our families and cultural and religious groups and some of us do   not. It takes courage to grow into ourselves.

Today builders are outside my window erecting a new roof and the scaffolding helps me see that coming to terms with my past as I write this memoir is providing the scaffolding and platform from which I can reclaim the old losses and also pick up the threads that were so much part of my true identity, but which I could not see at the time. I am becoming more whole and integrated in the writing of this memoir. I started from the perspective of giving self-expression to my *lost child* and have fallen into my *Authentic Self* as the process has progressed.

Yesterday I revisited the University College of London (UCL), in which The Slade School of Art is located and I remembered my days of study there as being the happiest of my life, in an environment where I could finally fit in.

It is a sunny Saturday lunchtime; students are on the lawns, just as I remember, and a memory comes to mind of a metal sculpture I made with bits of scrap metal, which I'd pop-riveted together. It was heavy and rough, with every part uneven and unlike anything I would have thought I could produce. I think, had I had more time, that I would have liked to have made it into the shape of a disc, representing the sun. However, as time was not on my side, I settled with an unfinished metal sculpture that had no overall

METAL SCULPTURE

shape, and I exhibited it those 25-years-ago, on the steps of the outbuilding that I am sitting right in front of. Maybe that sculpture was an unconscious attempt to put all the parts of myself together.

Louise Bourgeois, the artist said: **"We die of the past or we become an artist"**.

Making art was her way of dealing with her traumatic past, which haunted her throughout her life; but in making a piece of art she felt that she had some control over the original trauma, which had defeated her as a child. This feeling of being let down by her parents, who allowed her father's mistress to live in the family home as her *nanny*, creating the inspiration for her huge volume of work.

Early emotional neglect is an unconscious feeling held in the cells of the body of the *adult child* and it often goes unrecognised and hidden, behind a screen of the child's practical and material needs being met. The child may go to the best schools, own the best toys, have the best nannies, have successful parents, but if the emotional needs aren't met, often through no fault of the parents, who might have also been emotionally neglected themselves, the repercussions for the child in later adult life can be devastating. They might be hidden under the myth "my family life was perfect" and result in addictive behaviours such as alcohol, food, drugs, or the more socially acceptable addictive screens of work, busyness, high achievement and academic or material success – or the most recent one: social media. These are all respectable screens, and if taken to extreme, provide a numbing of the early colourless emotional palettes that drive the most successful people to possess everything but joy, satisfaction and vibrancy. This creates suffering, in the forms of depression, anxiety, self-harm and, in the worst of cases, suicide or homicide.

The "lost part of the Self" needs to come back to life in the wake of almost being stifled to death and to live in the joy of enthusiasm, spontaneity, liberation and self-knowledge, rather than the self-destructive drivenness or lethargy, leading to a reductive lifeforce energy that alienates us from our best potential within ourselves, our relationships and what we can create on the planet. In whatever way our external circumstances might present themselves, only we will know the truth of our inner landscape and often all might not be as it seems. In my own case, as mentioned earlier, the lies I told myself and held to be true were that I was well-meaning, when in fact I was judgemental and critical, but without owning it most of the time. I just disowned that part of myself as it was so entrenched in my habitual thinking.

Yesterday, at the UCL I was attending a conference on the theme of "The Good Life" in which one of the speakers was Dr. Rowan Williams, the ex Archbishop of Canterbury.

He spoke to my heart as his definition of *the good life* was:

"being at home in ourselves, in which we live towards a growing clarity which is not obsessed with the need to control the natural habitat of our lives. We tend the landscape of our inner world like a gardener planting and nurturing the seeds in his/her garden. We weed out the hostile destructive panics that shrink our world to a reactive precipice and look clearly at the passions of the soul. "Instinct unexamined," he states, "blocks our vision. We need the disciplines of intellect, imagination and attention" and he emphasises that we need to "be somewhere, to find a habitat; a place from which we can see. We need anchorage, a point of orientation within our body and surroundings. We can't depend on ourselves alone. Our identity is shaped by our rhythms, needs and self expressions being echoed and understood by dependable other/s. To be recognised makes for the good life," says Dr. Williams. "We need our story told back to us – not adrift under an empty sky". He says that "when we are at home within ourselves we have 'furniture' in our mind in which we can safely invite others and that the inner and outer environments relate. Living the 'good life' there is fresh rhythm, fresh reflection and generativity, our soul narrative", he says, "needs to be cared for and developed in order for us to move towards a 'good life'; not purely reactive but unifying our thinking and feeling. Bringing the mind into the heart; a constant flow of giving and receiving and attunement to the world it's in; a joyful attunement to reality. Being 'at home' in joy. The road to authenticity requires that we move beyond the known and disentangle our enmeshments. It can be painful and lonely at times as we always have to give up something in order to develop and grow."

In my own experience as with that of my clients, I can see that the personality disintegrates if the "truth of who we are" is not honoured and if the child is emotionally neglected and dismissed then the *authentic* part of its nature can get hidden and distorted and creates the False Self. Retrieving the Lost Child in the adult is not an easy journey and requires patience and perseverance because the False Self is well formed and believes the self-defeating and sometimes self-protective scripts that have developed over time. It is resistant to change because it has ruled the roost for most of our lives and so is hard to dismantle. Learning to embrace and celebrate my creative lifeforce energy has been a mission on my *authentic* life journey and I am now very grateful to be able to say "I am home, I have arrived, I am free.' I have learnt to turn self-defeating negatives such as: "I don't deserve to be loved, I'm a failure, I don't belong", into positives such as: I do deserve to be loved, I have succeeded and I do belong".

I found a letter today which fell into my hands from Kathleen, an art lecturer dated August 1993 at a weekend course I attended, which she facilitated at the very beginning of my journey as an artist, and it underlines the qualities that I was unable to see at the time, but which I feel has captured my very essence and echoes that sense of being seen and truly understood for the *authentic* being that I always was:

"You have a quasi-simple/quasi-complex artistic nature, with a gift for receptiveness & guidance. Your work is buoyant, expressive, vigorous and beautifully un-self-conscious. Whatever you do and however you do it in the future, maintain your individuality, choosing the colours, shapes and textures, and subject matter that inspire you towards self-expression. Your artwork will probably combine very successfully with your music and poetry, and the creative nature of your work. Disregard any pre-conceptions of "ARTIST"; just do it. You have no one to answer to, except an unidentified muse called FREEDOM – Every now and then, set yourself a little exercise eg. Draw a piece of crumpled paper for discipline (YOU DO NEED SOME PARAMETERS)."

This mirroring of my *True Self* – a sense of "all out personal aliveness," or "feeling real" was hidden to me in all other ways but through my creative expression and it is with gratitude that I had that possibility of connection. But now, 25-years on, I have retrieved that *lost child* in my deepest sense of *being*:

"the more we shine out in all of our human bitter sweetness, the more the fire of that light burns away the shame that causes us to hide. Shame is what keeps us in the dark, cowering, judging, and believing we are not enough. 'When we embody and speak our truth, that's when we are in our divinity, our freedom, liberation, spaciousness"

HeidiHindaChadwick

Interlude
Pause for Thought

ABSTRACT WINTER LANDSCAPE

It is Christmas Day 2017 and I have chosen to spend the day quietly in my small Highgate flat, where I have lived for the past forty years. I am approaching the end of my seventh decade. My home has been the most stable and consistent part of my life during this period, while I have gone through the various evolutions that inspire me to write this book.

As a Quaker Jewish Buddhist, it seems an appropriate way to Zen out on this Christmas Day, which has families gathered with all sorts of hidden, or not so hidden, agendas. I have taken an afternoon walk in Waterlow Park, North London, high above the city. It has always been a beautiful park and a sanctuary for my soul. As the winter daylight dims into dusk over the pond, the ducks are chasing each other, as are the dogs …so much chasing over this period … but not for me today the chase – just observing *being* and what presents itself. The trees are dancing in the soft breeze and I am being my *authentic self*. Always in the past thinking that I should be somewhere other than where I am or who I am; but not so today.

I am breathing
I am at peace
I am free

With no plans to the fore, I become inspired listening to Dame Janet Baker on the radio talking about her life. The renowned mezzo-soprano has always appealed to me and so it was an Xmas treat to hear her talk about her life as well as to hear her sing. Also good to hear and connect to some repertoire that I had sung in my studies as a singer some forty years ago, although my singing veered more towards comedy.

What appealed and inspired me was the knowledge that she knew her *authentic* path from as young as age nine. For me, however, it has been a constant and sometimes painful search to find my own. I can now see that the six decades of my life, through thick and thin, have brought me to where I am today with a sense of belonging to myself and to the world at long last.

Janet Baker talked of travelling in the States and how she would relax of an evening, savouring her voice by reading. "What sort of books?" asked the interviewer. This was an interesting question that appealed to the therapist side of myself. "Oh personal development, self-help books," she said. It was quite a surprising answer and it would seem that she never did overcome her feelings of terror before every performance, until her last. I was intrigued that she had to overcome these feelings each time she went on stage and yet it never deterred her from her chosen path and reaffirms to me the tremendous courage that is required to live authentically and pursue all that we feel called to do in our lives, in spite of the personal obstacles that we have to overcome.

It is evening and I hear a ring at the door. Not expecting anyone, I deliberate whether to answer or not and decide in the wake of my Zen day, that I will answer it. On the doorstep is a boyfriend from forty years ago. I was rather amused at this unexpected end to the day, only to find he was trying to convert me into the church of Christian Science, as if I didn't have enough in the way of spiritual conversion...

I am on the train to Sheffield on my way to a pre-New Year's Buddhist Retreat. I arrive at the hotel that I booked just around the corner from the Quaker Meeting House, where the retreat is to be held. Apparently due to a technical hitch, my booking had not been transferred. Eventually, error rectified, my room is ready and comfortable. Although I had asked for alarm calls on three consecutive days, they never arrive, due to another technical hitch. This, however, is instrumental in me having free breakfasts and experiencing a friendly spirit all around. When I tell the receptionist of my retreat she tells me how meditation had been the single most important change in her life.

WALKING MEDITATION

Back in my Highgate flat I am approaching the New Year's Eve countdown as 2017 draws to a close; the downstairs neighbour has offered me a last minute invitation before I head off to ring in and sing in the New Year with friends in Hampstead. I have gratefully accepted, just going along with the flow…

The New Year is a time for dreaming and I haven't ruled out having a mutually satisfying relationship with a heterosexual, bisexual or transgender person in my 70s, 80s or 90s but I have ruled out having children now.

This New Year I am celebrating my life with gratitude, appreciation and compassion. A life that has by no means been easy, but in looking back on the strange and wonderful roads I have walked I pay homage to that silent voice that lived deep within but could barely breathe in the shadow of suffocation; that silent voice that could only be expressed creatively through the means of art, poetry, imagination, song, dance, paint and the world of colour, which kept my soul alive when all else felt lost and dead. I now see that my creative expression was the language of my heart and a resting place for my soul.

Decade 8: Life Unfolding

(2018...)

After my seventieth birthday and in the pause between my actual birthday and my celebration, which was to be a multi-media event, I learnt that Sabine had died. I would not have known this, except for the fact that I received a call from another friend of Sabine's from some 20-years back. Jill, a friend from the past, had called me on the off chance that I would still be at the same address (that I was in 20-years ago and of course I was. She told me that Sabine had passed away. "It was peaceful", she said, "she died in her sleep, alone"...) I was shocked and glad at the same time – that it had been peaceful. I was glad but I was stunned. I found out later that she was discovered by her ex-husband.

Jill said that she would let me know of the funeral arrangements. I could let the celebrant know of any memories or thoughts to share as it was to be a Humanist funeral. I put the phone down and thought of Sabine dying alone and peacefully, which is exactly what she would have wanted. She couldn't have orchestrated it better.

Sabine, such a big presence in my life, even when we were not together, held a deal of my psychic energy whether together or apart. Our last call had been a confusing one, as all other calls *had* been over the past two years when I decided I could not fuel the friendship any more. Our last call happened a few months prior, and she was still holding on to the resentment that I had walked out on her some thirty years back. I said with frustration, "I cannot live in the past anymore Sabine – I have to live in the present". There was a pause and then I put the phone down, after asking her how she was, to no real reply.

We tried intermittently to continue a friendship, but it was always held that I had walked out on her, as did everyone else in her life; she made it an impossibility to stay. Hence she kept in touch with all her exes, safely at a distance, so that real relating could be avoided and there was always another one to get back in touch with. It seemed that some of the exes were flocking together in the wake of her passing, sharing writings with each other that we had all gathered over the years, which illustrated different facets of her life. During this period quite a synchronistic event happened around the time of her funeral.

I had been attending some theatre workshops over the past year, theatre having fallen away from my life some thirty years ago, but an opportunity had presented itself that I found too tempting to turn my back on, and there I was doing improvisations around body image, food and self-esteem, based on the writings of Susie Orbach's iconic book *Fat is a Feminist Issue*. One of the participants happened to be one of Sabine's exes, she had ex's everywhere. I later found out, as I put two and two together from a telltale sign in her improvisation. I introduced myself to her and asked if she knew someone called Sabine, to which she looked amazed, and replied that she did. I told her of Sabine's death and of the funeral that I was to attend just that week. The cosmos seemed to be interweaving connections and putting some of us together in uncanny ways; she told me that she had some writing of Sabine's, as did I, and we exchanged them the following week; strangely comforting as threads of the tapestry were being pulled together from different women, different ex's, different perspectives.

Sabine's first female lover was Michelle Causse, a feminist writer who had introduced Sabine to the female writers of the day in Paris. This must have been an intoxicating period for Sabine and her relationship with Michelle had meant everything to her in those days of escape from family. She talked fondly of the spinach patch on the ceiling left by hurtling a plate high up during a row and I'm informed that there were many, but they had run away together, sharing their intimate vulnerabilities and love in a one room garret studio in the heart of the Left Bank, indulged by a stimulating array of world renowned writers, artists and film directors of the time.

Sabine must have been in her element; histrionics, hysteria, hilarity and drama being at the very root of her essence. However her relationship with Michelle was not to last as she left Sabine_to join another female lover in Rome some seven years into the relationship and this was to leave Sabine devastated.

I believe she never recovered from this first abandonment and any relationship after that was an impossibility. I had intense feelings for her vulnerability, as on some level it matched my own and my own need for an outward show of histrionics, hysteria, hilarity and drama as I had no other way to express my feelings, which met a home from home within the framework of our relationship.

Sabine was an advocate for an unhealthy philosophy in life; she liked being indirect, living in the past or future but never in the present, contrary to many spiritual evocations and I kept pushing for that impossibility; a relationship with direct communication. So wherever we travelled in the world, and we did a lot of travelling together, I was always left with the pain of disconnection. In looking at it now through the eyes of my role as *the therapist* I can see that maybe the pain of disconnection is what I expected from a relationship, as true relating required intimacy and I believe that both of us craved what we couldn't give each other; the inner losses being too great; and so we endured a never-ending long and winding road in and out of relationship and friendship.

Now it was my seventieth birthday celebration. So with a mixed bag of feelings I approached the day with consolation that it was as much for myself as others. I had been given the whole of the vegan cabaret restaurant next door to my studio for my thirty guests to eat, be entertained by a screening of my one-woman show from the '80s: – *Take Off with Mrs. Frumburger*, and a cabaret with acts provided by my guests. It was an ambitious programme but I was orchestrating it from an *authentic* need to pull some of the threads of my life together, trusting that it would all take care of itself. It was slightly chaotic with some guests arriving late and some after the event had more or less finished, but all was ok with my new feeling of just being at peace with the flow of things as they are…

As the screening of **Mrs. Frumburger** commenced some guests had to leave including the 1960's/70's folk musicians who were going to provide the entertainment; but all was not lost and we continued some two weeks later, completing the ceremonials in the Quaker meeting house.

Although living seventy years on this earth has left many boxes unticked, I realise that I have lived an uncompromising and unusual life. I had prepared a finely chiselled speech for after the meal, and before the film of *Frumburger*, which went down far better at home than at the party to an audience of distracted eating and drinking friends as there was no neat end to the eating and we were so behind schedule from the start. I took an unsteady step off the stage and back to my table, feeling a little disorientated. I find now I am more and more needing quiet times, and socialising is really quite an effort… even at my own party.

A week on at the crematorium I looked out for a woman with a big hat, who I recognise to be Jill. We sat on a bench in the sun sharing our experiences and stories about Sabine. She was left with feelings of guilt, as she had not been in touch with her for many years, and was left with exotic fantasies of how they might have had tea in Fortnum's sporting large hats, talking and sharing about feminist French and American writers, little knowing that Sabine had stopped being stylish many years back and preferred, rather, to dress more like a *who cares* teenager, with a baseball hat replacing her trilby and a *two fingers up* attitude to match.

I had particularly found the *Sabine. with attitude* difficult to be with, contrary to Jill, who was still living with the Sabine from the past. As I was becoming a Therapist, which was not to Sabine's liking, a fortnight being long term therapy for her, who came away from sessions with more information about the inadequacies of the Therapist than focusing on her own vulnerabilities. I was also beginning to honour myself within a relationship more, and could no longer pretend, something that I had excelled at most of my life when it came to relating. We were at loggerheads.

The service was rather beautiful considering that Sabine believed that no one would attend her funeral. It was hard for her to understand that people did care, but she screened out the world with her prickly defensiveness, which left her in that same uncomfortable space of no one being there for her. Her son and grandson and ex-husband of some 51-years of intermittent relationship, paid homage, as did a fully tattooed man from her Italian group, neighbours, a home help attempting to educate Sabine into the world of computers, and myself, Jill, and the celebrant, who had concocted a compilation of Sabine's life, from poetry, written memories and drawings – an altogether very sincere tribute. We completed proceedings by taking tea at her ex-husband's, in the same house that she had lived in with him some 45 years previously. A common theme presented itself: how all who were close had to close down communications on and off, because Sabine was so inclined to invade other's lives and vulnerabilities and invent a scenario of her own that left one feeling unguarded; her own vulnerabilities controlled by medicating her migraines with painkillers on a regular basis.

My feelings were rather confused after the funeral – beautiful and sincere but also rather lost within everyone else's group experiences and reminiscences and my relationship seemingly drowned out, as in life it had been.

In the days that followed, however, I could at last acknowledge my own relationship with Sabine, and the love that I felt, but could not express in real life, although I had tried. She had negated our relationship in holding that I had left and abandoned her. My own perspective could come back into play that it was the most significant relationship in my life; and have not experienced such a poignant one since. It was a great relief to finally be able to relive the good memories again and leave the painful ones behind. Why I was attracted to her in the first place; her sense of beauty, language, culture, art and fun. I felt free again and I felt Sabine's soul had also been liberated. This line came to me while sitting in silence at a Quaker meeting for worship:

'all loose threads lead somewhere'

I know that Sabine. was greatly inspired by the *Tibetan Book of Dying*, later retitled *The Tibetan Book of Living and Dying* and I went on a mini-retreat over the weekend to educate myself. I am glad to have the new version within my grasp as an aid to further my journey as I live my life more transparently and authentically. I am glad to be reaching out and exploring the world of other people more fully now than I ever have before, because for me it is the most unlived part of my life and quite contrary to the attachment needs of a human being. Moments of connection with others help me to believe that human connection *is* a possibility and that I can embrace more and more intimacy as I learn to trust myself and honour my own needs in this respect.

It is March 2019 and I find myself back on stage, treading the boards with a troop of feminist thespians in a production called *How Am I Looking Now?*, the result of all those drama workshops, with an all ages female cast looking at issues around self-esteem and body image; a glorious, tragic romp full of outrageous surprises. Because the subject matter brings so much anger to the surface, director/writer, Clair Chapwell decides that using humour and music is the best way of highlighting the issues around body image, self-acceptance and self-esteem, since issues now are so much more pronounced with the advent of social media and young women's need to acquire the perfect body by whatever means, whether plastic surgery to the face, genitalia or other parts.

Question and answer sessions were held after some shows with the audience and we were on one occasion joined by Susie Orbach. Chapwell had written *Baring the Weight* in 1979 staged by her theatre company, Spare Tyre, based around Orbach's book *Fat is a Feminist Issue* and we performed both shows by way of comparison. How have things changed in 40 years?

"The three months of rehearsals for 17 women from a variety of backgrounds and cultures aged from 22 to 74 yielded the wonderful feeling of intergenerational closeness. As strong as the show made us feel, as positive and powerful, we were aware that many aspects of the world remains a hostile place for women, keen to keep our anxiety about body image simmering, just as it was 40 years ago, to Orbach's great despair. How to confront these forces that surround us?"

Let us all know that we are enough, however we look, feel or think because we are alive on this planet at this time, all of us *just learning.*

SOME OF THE CAST '*HOW AM I LOOKING NOW?*' MARCH 2019 (ISA IS IN THE FRONT ROW IN RED)

Lawn of Memories

On this summer's evening

the gentleness of aloneness

the stillness of silence.

Only the magpie hops across the lawn at a great pace

where the children had blown ephemeral bubbles.

Grandma played with grandchild

Young boys kicked footballs that I tried to retrieve

from under my bench,

always out of reach.

The beauty of the walled border flowers, wild yet tamed by artistry

This lawn where I entertained with jazz song

Where thespians ran riot a la Shakespeare

The lawn where mother, father, friends, lovers, relations

Lie lost to life

All are with me now in this sweet twilight silence

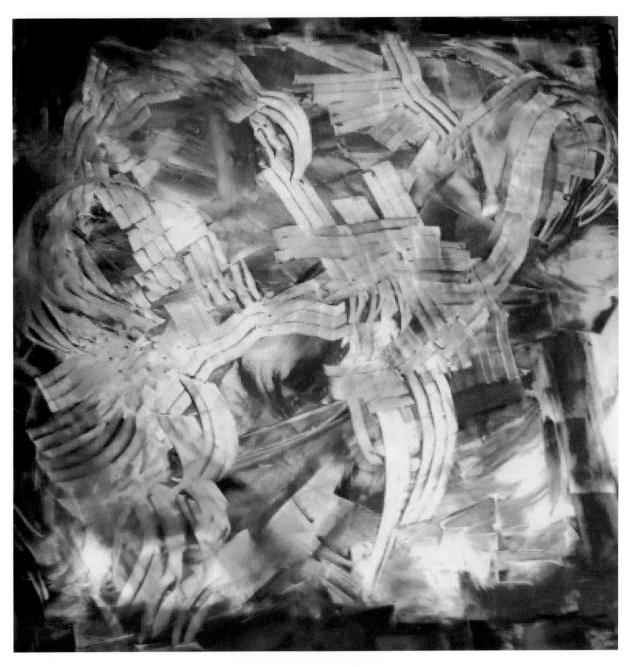

ABSTRACT LANDSCAPE

Epilogue

As I face the "Female Resurrection" for a final conversation with it, I am becoming aware that the legacy of guilt that I went through in coming to terms with the painting of it has also been a turning point in transcending my own suffering. If I look at the Celtic cross, I can truly identify with it. The four sides are:

*Self

*Wisdom

*Divine God/Goddess

*Nature

This being so I can embrace my journey of wholeness beyond the tribal and into the realms of the divine, with the hope that the world can marry the material with the mystical and as I face the canvas I hear its voice saying softly:

You are a non-conformist woman who wears the multi-coloured
cloak of Evolution;
You are You
Alive and free
Go share your fruits and blossoms
Of Hope and Possibility
Each to the Other
Rich, at Peace and Abundant
You are You
Alive and free
You are You

My hope is that the world can also find a way to transcend the material and find a way to marry the needs for material sustenance with the needs for the more mystical connections to the Divine Feminine in our world whether it be within the male or female of our species, which has been so sadly missing within our patriarchal systems. The power of the Divine is within us all male and female, and switched into this power our world would be enriched beyond recognition, each shining their light onto the planet, rather than looking to some other authority for our power.

In contrast, as we approach the deadline for Brexit, those in power have never been so exposed for the tribal infighting, backbiting and the very worst that patriarchal power has created.

PLANT & TULIPS

In this chaos we are asked to make decisions that no one knows the answer to and as the conditioning within our tribal systems is falling apart, we hold on even tighter to we know not what, in the belief that one way is better than another.

I now have hope for a more balanced and harmonious world where the traditionally accepted forces of corruption in places of power will be challenged as each human being becomes more empowered by their own divine light and not the voice of the systems dictating rules contrary to divine nature but inclusive of it.

While there is a tree and a human breath there is hope

References

Winnicott, D. Healing the Fragmented Selves of
Trauma Survivors (Da Capo Press) (1992)

Yukavitch, L. The Misfit's Manifesto (Simon & Shuster)
(2019)

Gibran, K. The Prophet (Simon & Shuster) (2020)

Maitreya's Teachings, The Law of Life
Edited by **Benjamin Creme** (2005)

Tolle, E. The Power of Now (Namaste Publishing) (1997)

Scott-Peck, M. The Road Less Travelled
 Touchstone) (2003)

Bourgeois, L. Intimate Geometries:
The Art and Life of Louise Bourgeoise (Monacelli Press) (2014)

Chadwick, Heidi Hinda The Creative Genius (2019)

Isa L Levy MA

Isa is both a performing and a visual artist. Her acting career includes repertory and touring theatre of the British Isles, and fringe theatre in both London and Edinburgh. Her TV career culminated in her appearing as a Bride of Dracula on the BBC's comedy *The Dave Allen Show*. She has also devised, written and performed her comedy One-Woman shows, which included a performance for life sentence prisoners in HMP Wormwood Scrubs, this was covered by BBC Radio 4 Woman's Hour. It was her final performance for 30 years before she took to the boards again in 2019 acting in a musical fringe production entitled: *How Am I Looking Now?* This show was performed in London and based on Susie Orbach's book of the '80s, *Fat is a Feminist Issue.* It compares women's body issues now, in this age of social media, with those issues in the '80s. In the same year, she was invited by her local MP to perform a song, she wrote some 50 years ago, in parliament during a climate crisis rally stressing the urgency for politicians to act now.

In the '90s Isa discovered a talent for painting, having had no past experience, and produced some 450 paintings in many different styles and subjects. She ended up at The Slade School of Fine Art with a bursary from Equity (the Actors Union). Isa has exhibited internationally and held solo exhibitions in London over a 15-year-period, including the Ben Uri Gallery's Fortnight of Solo Artists Exhibition, where she featured in their 2007 Diary. She was selected as a finalist in the East/West Arts Award Exhibition in the West End's, La Galleria in Pall Mall, London. Her latest exhibition was at St Martin-in-the-Fields, Trafalgar Square, where she exhibited with two other women Quaker artists, who had different religious backgrounds. During this time Isa facilitated *Art for All* workshops for children, adults and women ex-offenders in London, France and Italy. As this intense chapter closed she realised she had no more paintings to paint and she needed to share her story of all she had learnt in the process of facing all those "blank canvasses".

In the new Millennium, Isa proceeded to do her Masters in Arts Psychotherapy without an A Level to her name. Isa is now a practising Arts Psychotherapist working from her

About the author continues on opposite page…

About the author continued….

Highgate consultancy. While still a trainee, she and other trainees set up a project at Islington Mind where clients could be treated promptly.

Email: isalevy@aol.com

Paintings / Studio Visits: www.isalevy.co.uk

Arts Psychotherapy: www.isalouiselevyartspsychotherapist.co.uk

Website: www.conversationswithablankcanvas.com

YouTube Isa Levy: Different Lives: https://youtu.be/YOMlxAxVmjl

YouTube Isa Levy: Conversations with a Blank Canvas: https://youtu.be/I0Hq6LWA8yl

The song Isa participated in *Love Will Find A Way* https://youtu.be/qnUiRRYrpvg

Book Reviews

"I literally could not put this book down. It is beautifully written. The author shares an honest, detailed and thought provoking self assessment of her life journey. It is reflective in ways which invite the reader to engage more consciously with their own personal journey. Using wonderfully clear and apt word painting, the words are beyond poetic in that they evoke a reaction of all our senses. We hear the music she created, we feel the gentle opening up within the lover's garden, and we even taste the mother's force feeding!

This is a remarkable achievement which leads us to a deeper level of engagement with the text. Rather than it being an observed memoir of an other life, the experience is offered to us as a sharing. From within the kitchen of her own creativity, we share a meal of self discovery, self-enrichment and a certainty that the author has no preconceived expectations of our response. We are asked only to be authentic in her presence, as she is in ours.

This is real, and we are asked to respond to it from our own individual reality.

That said, it also has moments of great humour – the Mothers' behaviour towards police, and traffic wardens is to be treasured. The stage lost a great comic actress when Isa Louise Levy decided that she needed to change direction. Finally, I am convinced that, had she truly wanted to, she could have sold a kitchen! "

Frances Sutherland

"It takes a lot of guts to do what Isa has done: to look at a blank canvas. We all have our own blank canvases: our lives. We all have the ability and power to put something on that canvas, but it takes great bravery to make the first brushstroke and then eventually look at the finished painting. Then we must interpret what it is saying to us. Isa teaches us a great deal about her own life, but also about our own lives too.

From the experience gathered through her decades of being a child, actor, salesperson, artist and psychotherapist, with enormous courage Isa takes us through her life and explores its meaning. There are ups and downs, pluses and minuses, positives and negatives, issues to be faced, and we can all identify with her journey and contemplate what we can learn from it on a personal level. For example, how did our own upbringings affect us? How might we come into our authentic selves? How can we bring our personal talents to life? How can we make the most of our own "blank canvases"? At the end of it all, we can all be resurrected in our talented aliveness and we offer Isa great thanks for this enlightenment. "

Joanna Godfrey Wood

"Isa`s book is treasure chest. She is not only describing her lifelong journey in an open and heartwarming way, it is also full of profound insights and inspirations for one`s own journey!"

Dieter Langenecker

Book Reviews continues on opposite page…

Book Reviews continued …

"*Conversations with a Blank Canvas is a beautiful, brave and compelling autobiographical work. The power of the memoir is evident at both a micro and macro level. The author affords us an understanding of her own deeply personal and very individual experience of life, and in doing so creates a seductive invitation to review and reflect upon our own, exploring universal themes of belonging, acceptance and Self. Isa Levy's creative works – poetry, prose and art, all referenced in the memoir – display a raw personal vulnerability as well as a deep sense of knowing around these potent and relevant themes. In these current times of uncertainty 'Conversations with a Blank Canvas' could not be more relevant, as an invitation to each of us to use this pause in life to review and reflect upon what we have felt, what is real for us and what we can do to guide our own personal trajectory. As one woman's reflection upon her own life it is indeed a ...celebration of life, complexity and freedom.*"

Maia

"*The word 'self' is understood and used by nearly all people. It occurs as part of frequently heard expressions such as, for example, 'I myself would never understand mathematics' or 'He himself admitted he hated doing the washing up' or 'Isn't it about time you learnt to do your tax return by yourself?' Alternatively, we can the use the word 'self' in a descriptive way when calling someone self-centred or selfless or indeed selfish.*

In her book 'Conversations with a Blank Canvas' Isa Levy writes about 'self' in a different, profound and important way, one in which many of us never consider doing. This is because most of us just get on with life and even if they feel something is wrong or missing in their lives they never ponder what it is that feels 'wrong'.

For Isa Levy there were many things from an early age that felt desperately 'wrong', made her unhappy and feel that she didn't fit in anywhere in the world. Eventually, in her 20s she realised she didn't know who she really was, and began to wonder if she had a 'true self'. The answer seemed to be a resounding 'no'.

Reading her account of how she managed to achieve a 'true self' is reading about someone who courageously journeyed from childhood 'emotional imprisonment' to the freedom of getting in touch with these long lost feelings and starting to feel an autonomous person, alive and of value. Isa gives a vivid account of how unwittingly her parents never acknowledged her needs, feelings and abilities, or denied them to a point she lost track of them herself. Unknowingly, she had suffered what psychotherapists call emotional abuse and neglect. That Isa was able to learn about herself in the most unusual ways makes her book a treatise on hope and determination which will be of help to anyone who has suffered doubts about their identity and value as a person. For those who have not had to battle with such issues, Isa Levy's book will provide an intensely moving account of an amazing and almost unimaginable journey.

Dr Sue Van Colle BA (Hons) Dip MT (Roehampton) PhD

Copyright

PAT DEVEREAUX
PUBLISHING WORKS
patdevereaux@mac.com

Conversations with a Blank Canvas

Printed in Great Britain
by Amazon